BRAND NEW CHURCH?

BRAND NEW CHURCH?

The church and the postmodern condition

Graeme Fancourt

First published in Great Britain in 2013

Society for Promoting Christian Knowledge
36 Causton Street
London SW1P 4ST
www.spckpublishing.co.uk

British Library Cataloguing-in-Publication Data
A catalogue record for this book is available from the British Library

ISBN 978–0–281–06797–8
eBook ISBN 978–0–281–06798–5

Typeset by Graphicraft Limited, Hong Kong
First printed in Great Britain by Ashford Colour Press
Subsequently digitally printed in Great Britain

eBook by Graphicraft Limited, Hong Kong

Produced on paper from sustainable forests

For Amy, Millie and Olivia

'Writing turns you into somebody who's always wrong. The illusion that you may get it right someday is the perversity that draws you on.'

Philip Roth, *American Pastoral*

Contents

Acknowledgements

I am enormously grateful to the English Speaking Union, whose American Memorial Chapel Scholarship enabled me to travel to the USA to carry out the American side of this research project. Thanks are also due to the kind grants made by the Lady Hewley Trust, the Baptist Union of Great Britain and the Church of England Ministry Division.

My doctoral supervisors, the Revd Prof. David Wilkinson and the Revd Dr Gavin Wakefield, were bricks during my four years at Durham, and I shall always be thankful for their patience and wisdom, enabling me finally to make some sense. Some.

There are too many people who participated in this research project to list by name, but my thanks to you all for the generosity you showed with your time, and for the honesty and integrity you demonstrated in our meetings together. I am also grateful to Prof. Tom Beaudoin of Fordham University, and to the members of his graduate and ministry classes with whom I met and from whom I gained so much.

My thanks are also owed to Alison Barr at SPCK, whose highly tuned, plain-speaking editing skills and support have been enormously helpful in the writing of this book.

The Parish of Caversham Thameside and Mapledurham is my clerical stomping ground, and what a lovely bunch of fellow stompers they are too! My incumbent was kind enough to give me the time to carry out this research, and to write this book; I promise that I will now get back to work.

Acknowledgements

Finally, I am utterly indebted to my wife, Amy, and to my children, Millie and Olivia, who have supported me beyond all reason in the years that have led to the writing of this book. You have made all the difference.

1

Why bother with the postmodern condition?

I'm told that cooking a frog can be quite a tricky business. Attempt to put it in a pan of boiling water and it will, apparently, hop straight back out. Instead, the chef should place the frog in cold water, where the little chap will merrily swim around. Only then should the heat be turned on, so that the frog slowly, gently, falls asleep, unaware of what is to become of it.

Without taking the analogy too far, I would like to suggest that we all grow up being gently 'cooked' in the waters of family and local practice; national identity and history; global technological, political and economic change. Of course maturity, education and travel may alter one's perspective, and it is possible to become more deeply aware of the way people and institutions operate, but none of us ever understands completely all that has gone into making us who we are.

It is a small step from considering how we are affected by sociocultural 'cooking', to asking how this may have impacted the church. Indeed, debates on this topic have raged from the days of St Paul onwards. Some have maintained that the church is good news because it is uniquely resistant to its surroundings, and offers peace and safety. Others would dismiss this position as unreal escapism and argue that the church is good news only when it is incarnate within society and culture. But might becoming incarnate (a) cause the church to lose its distinctiveness and integrity, and (b) indicate a loss of faith in the church's own beliefs and practices? Could it reduce the church to just another player in political and cultural popularity contests? This book ponders what the church is called to be in the contemporary Western world – a world that bears striking similarities to the ancient world while also being enormously different.

Today we live in a high-octane, high-speed, non-stop, credit-fuelled blast, trying to make the most of every moment we've got. We are deeply influenced by technological and free-market advances that no one could have dreamed of a hundred years ago. The last century has seen an obsession with 'big projects' – attempts to bring unity, civilization or peace to the whole world, to improve trade and to make money. Western colonial expansion, international missionary movements, and the rise and domination of multinational companies are all examples of these big projects. Any hope that such efforts would bring peace or unity to the world, however, died in the course of two world wars. Generations have been left questioning why these big projects failed so spectacularly in their aims when those projects have succeeded in advancing technology and increasing wealth. Indeed, there is now a discernible attitude of cynicism directed towards all big projects, whether political or religious: everything is vanity and greed. This mix of technological optimism and political cynicism is very much a part of what I later define as 'the postmodern condition', and with which this book is concerned.

Over the last six years, I have travelled around the UK and USA to ask various church leaders their views on the church and the postmodern condition, and what kinds of things their churches are up to. It has been a fascinating and encouraging experience: the church that I have encountered is thoughtful, active and confident in the gospel. Despite many reports of its terminal decline in the Western media, if the church leaders I have met with are representative of the whole, then the church has good reason to be hopeful about its future. Though holding many different views, these leaders all appear to take seriously the need for the church genuinely to engage (positively or negatively) with what it perceives to be the postmodern condition.

In the course of the book, I also reflect on commentaries on the Western church and relevant works of contemporary theology. By engaging with the kind of thinking found both in local churches and in theological colleges and universities, I hope the reflections that emerge will be neither impractical nor superficial.

I will begin in this chapter by defining what I mean by the postmodern condition (it really isn't as complicated as it sounds), explaining why I use that particular term, and why I think it matters. In Chapter 2 I will review the way other writers have recently attempted to explain the church in the contemporary West through their engagement with the 'emerging church' movement. Whatever one's view on the emerging church, the discussions around this movement serve as a focus for questions about the church and the postmodern condition, and help identify various positions. This chapter also offers an explanation and evaluation of the way the emerging church movement has been presented and defined by various writers.

The third chapter is an edited collection of six transcripts from meetings I have had with church leaders in the UK and USA, presented as a single conversation. Reflecting on the understandings of the relationship between the church and the postmodern condition presented by these church leaders, as well as the writers presented in Chapter 2, enables me to describe what I see in the church today. Chapter 4 offers a map of how the church relates in different ways to the postmodern condition, showing where the church is in conflict with the postmodern condition, where it is in dialogue, and where it is in danger of surrendering its very nature in order to be popular. The last two chapters then argue why 'dialogue' is the most appropriate and enriching way for the church to understand itself: the fifth explains more specifically how this 'dialogue' functions, while the sixth suggests what this church-in-dialogue looks like in practice.

What is the postmodern condition?

I understand 'the postmodern condition' (also the title of a book, of which more in a moment) to be made up of two concepts: postmodern-ism and postmodern-ity. Both are broadbrush attempts to explain a complex of issues, but they are quite effective shorthand. 'Postmodern-ity' refers to the social, cultural, political and economic changes that the world has seen over the past few decades, leading to a greater sense of individualism, a 'smaller' world with 'less' time, and a greater focus upon free-market capitalism. 'Postmodern-ism' is a philosophical term describing attempts to ask what one may know, while questioning many claims to truth. It is a far more complicated and contested term than can be summed up by 'relativism' or 'pluralism', even if these are important elements within postmodernism. In order to make my own view as clear as possible, I will briefly outline some of the work of four thinkers associated with the postmodern condition.

Jean Baudrillard

While he wasn't the first to use the term, Jean Baudrillard is a thinker most closely associated with the concept of the postmodern condition. This is partly due to associations made between his work and the *Matrix* movies (much to Baudrillard's disapproval), and partly because N. T. Wright often refers to Baudrillard as an exemplar of the postmodern condition.[1] Through his playful and pessimistic social commentaries, Jean Baudrillard presents his view of a world that has become 'hypermodern'. When reading his work, there are times when one wonders if he is employing a cutting irony or making a serious philosophical enquiry, not that he would necessarily wish to separate the two, or even recognize these categories as valid. With this in mind, it is always dangerous to take Baudrillard at his word; proof-texting his work in order to define the postmodern condition is definitely out.

Baudrillard's presentation of hypermodernity is an attempt to say that all of humanity has been reduced to nothing more than a gaggle of zombies who mindlessly respond to anything that stimulates them.[2] Such is their reliance upon the media, these zombies really only experience the world through the way media simulates it, rather than experiencing the world itself. These media simulations of reality are said to project a world that is godless and solely focused upon capital gain. I find this all quite depressing and wouldn't recommend it as bedtime reading: existence is reduced to nothing more than consumption, for the whole world has become a giant supermarket in which humanity is condemned to walk mindlessly round circular aisles that go everywhere yet lead nowhere, shopping for spectacular-looking objects that will never deliver their promises.[3]

It's difficult not to regard Baudrillard's presentation as somewhat simplistic, but if not taken literally, his 'hyper-reality' can be appreciated for the imaginative suggestions it makes about how powerful the media can be in engrossing and absorbing one's views of the world, and how one acts within it.

David Harvey

Like Baudrillard, David Harvey has a negative view of the postmodern condition, seeing it as an insidious, nihilistic 'swamp'[4] that allows consumerism complete control over all thinking and doing. Unlike Baudrillard, however, he writes in order to save people from this repression. Harvey is a 'social geographer' who is also a Marxist, and believes that only through such a big project as Marxism can the free market be curbed from profiteering in all spheres of human life.[5]

For Harvey, the postmodern condition is in direct opposition to Marxism: arising from the desire to increase personal wealth,[6] technology has been developed to the point where it has compressed time and space. This is to say that because a person can physically travel the world in days, not years, can communicate instantly across the globe, and can employ technological developments to do more in a working day, then the world is experienced as smaller and time as shorter than it was just a few decades ago. While this could potentially have led to spending less time 'at work', the fact that this whole project has been driven by the desire to make money means people spend just as much time at work, getting more done in the same amount of time, and so making more money.

Looking at the postmodern condition from his Marxist perspective, Harvey is concerned at the way relativism has gained such a dominant voice that the big projects (such as Marxism or Christianity) that have a solution for the world are treated as arrogant. This relativism has become so widespread, he believes, that those who are 'different' from oneself are treated as sharing nothing in common at all. Harvey stands firm on his Marxist principles and challenges both of these assumptions. First, saying that big projects are invalid because they claim a unique understanding of truth is nonsense, as such a standpoint is in itself a truth-claim, attempting to argue that there is no truth. Harvey believes that this invalidates such postmodern posturing,[7] and so does not provide a strong enough argument as to why a big project cannot be an appropriate response to the postmodern condition. The confrontation of falsehood with the truth is the only appropriate response to the postmodern condition, and allows Harvey to do that which Baudrillard claims is futile: to go behind the media representations of the world in order to formulate a true representation of reality.[8]

This can be seen more fully in his second criticism: that the postmodern condition applies the term 'difference' as a cynical ploy for greater domination by the rich.[9] If another person, or group of people, can be said to be so different from me that there is no common humanity between us, then that person or group is a different species. Such an understanding of the world, suggests Harvey, allows the rich to continue living in their own world, unaffected by the world of the poor. But this is grossly inhuman, and Harvey wishes to see people liberated out of such unfairness. He believes this can happen through a new form of Marxism that offers hope to those who have been enslaved by the technological developments and capitalist expansion of the rich.[10]

While David Harvey's criticisms of the postmodern condition rightly point to an ethical vacuum at the heart of much postmodern enquiry, they do so in a way that suggests that the 'big project' approach is the only viable alternative. One needs to question why Harvey so forcibly insists on this. All big projects rely upon a 'big story' to present the vision of where a project is leading the world. Postmodern criticism of such projects not only questions their truth-claims, but also highlights their poor track record: do big projects ever deliver on their claims? Further, there is a strong argument that these big projects are simply a cover for one group's attempt to dominate the world at the expense of others.

Given that Marxism depends upon the big story of liberating the masses, one can see why postmodernism is proving to be a particular threat. In Harvey's work, Marxism and postmodern thought are presented as a clash of desires for the world, and Harvey attempts to show the postmodern condition as the less powerful of the two. In following this approach, however, he is not fully able to engage with the critique that big projects and stories are held in disdain by many people, not necessarily because of any commitment to capitalism, but because there is genuine concern that they inappropriately impose foreign value systems and, even more seriously, are simply fantasies. Here, though, is the rub: Harvey cannot fully engage with these criticisms because to do so would mean he would have to hold to the possibility that Marxist liberation is something less than a universal truth. Harvey uncompromisingly lives within a particular story, and his hope is that others will recognize the futility of capitalism in any of its forms, and join him.

Jean-François Lyotard

At one time a member of a revolutionary Marxist group in Algeria, Lyotard rejected Marxism as just another Western attempt to tell the world how to live. Many years later, in 1979, in a succinct and simple work, he dared to attempt to define the postmodern condition and so ignite the imaginations of others who were equally disenchanted with big projects. In a term that is often misquoted, Lyotard defined the postmodern as 'incredulity toward metanarratives',[11] which, rather than being a denial of their existence, is an expression of exhaustion and indifference in the face of the big stories that were intended to lead all of humanity and the world into a great Enlightenment, but were perceived to be failing.

Throughout his work on the postmodern condition, Lyotard repeats his claim that the big projects that seek to make the world conform to particular standards and live according to a certain understanding of reality are either mythical, violent, or both. Rather than choosing to live within the least evil project, or to do nothing, Lyotard calls his readers to be 'witnesses to the unpresentable'.[12] What he means by this is to live in a very hopeful manner, resisting the assumption that the powerful will continue to be powerful, and instead seeking after the emergence of forgotten, sidelined or new ways of being. This is to adopt a position of 'paralogy', which Lyotard defines as moving against the established methods of reasoning.[13] Doing so, however, may involve difficulty in understanding postmodern thought, as it attempts to express itself in ways that can seem strange.[14]

Lyotard's advocating of paralogy contradicts David Lyon's usually very helpful commentary on the philosopher that he 'sidesteps the question of social transformation'.[15] What Lyotard is suggesting is not a progressive transformation in a Marxist sense, but a focus upon what the powerful centre has marginalized so that it may be re-presented. It is this 'paralogy' that is transformative, not as a prescribed action, but as a way of being in relation to, of *resisting*, the big stories peddled by those in power. This point is highlighted by Lyotard in an interview he gave in his later years, in which he insisted that 'what we have to resist is at bottom despair and surrender',[16] which are the effects of these big projects.

In this sense, the postmodern condition is not merely a novelty, or playing for the sake of play, as it is often unfairly caricatured. According to Lyotard, those who occupy a postmodern position challenge those in power, and their claims to truth, so that the forgotten, silenced, ignored and new are able to (re-)emerge. The modern and the postmodern, then, are not references to old and new, but exist together: that which is honoured, and that which is marginalized or yet to be discovered.[17]

The question that remains unanswered, however, is how paralogy itself resists becoming a big project, and whether it is simply anarchy by another name. If this is the case, then David Lyon's criticism regarding a lack of interest in social transformation may, in part, be justified, as such a state of 'paralogy' could lead to paralysis by confusion, rather than any action upon the big projects that are thought to be so destructive. Furthermore, Lyon quite rightly follows Bruno Latour in saying that Lyotard, and many other postmodern philosophers, wrongly 'assume that modernity is a seamless all-enveloping environment'.[18] Not only does 'modernity' have a number of different and differing big projects and stories, but those projects themselves are often much more diverse and far less certain of themselves than the way in which they are presented by postmodern criticism. Lyon states that it is more appropriate to suggest that 'modernity has lived with inner doubts and contradictions from the start.'[19]

This criticism, though, only applies to Lyotard to a point. While he certainly does present the modern condition as an attempt to force everybody into a particular project, he is also careful to illustrate that the postmodern condition has always existed alongside this. There have always been those who question the wish to unify the world according to their own way of seeing it. This, perhaps, helps to explain Lyotard's presentation of the modern and the postmodern as two co-existent movements. Whereas the former is the movement to unify or liberate humanity at whatever cost, the latter is the movement against the flaws and self-confidence inherent within such projects.[20]

Zygmunt Bauman

Sociologist Zygmunt Bauman, a Polish immigrant who has lived and worked in northern England since 1972, has written prolifically on 'liquid modernity' since his retirement in 1990. Like Lyotard, Bauman has been a committed Marxist and communist, although Bauman continues to comment upon Western society and globalization from a socialist perspective.[21] 'Liquid modernity' is Bauman's explanation of the postmodern condition: an evocative metaphor for how loyalties to aristocracy or family structures, as well as obligations to institutions, have melted into the air. 'Solid modernity' held confidence in 'society' as a fair and just arbiter of life so that one's identity could be worked towards and earned. Liquid modernity, however, is like 'an Escher universe, where no one, at no point, can tell the difference between a way uphill and a descending slope'.[22] Solid modernity allowed people to work towards their dreams, and such work gave them an identity. Liquid modernity is focused on consumerism rather than work, so that identities are constructed through the things one buys and wears and uses, rather than what one does. In this society, capitalism 'is stronger, and can look forward to a favoured future'.[23]

Within this consumerist society, happiness is never a state that one can achieve, as there is always more to purchase and collect. This means that the 'state' of happiness is actually replaced by the 'pursuit' of happiness, and as the nature of a pursuit is endless, this forces individuals to play a game they can never win.[24] As the state of happiness is an impossible dream, the 'hope of becoming happy' is that which drives individuals to dress themselves in signs and symbols of happiness. Just like a child with a football card collection, the more one is able to collect, and the more sought-after the items, the happier one will be.[25]

This consumerist understanding of human personhood is, for Bauman, an unwelcome social development that has led to 'spinelessness' in the way people deal with their own identities and beliefs.[26] The pursuit of happiness, it would seem, comes at the cost of one's soul, portions of which can be temporarily leased to the highest bidders. In contrast to this self-centred approach to life, Bauman suggests that the liberation from social structures within liquid modernity allows human persons to make genuinely free, moral choices to seek their happiness in another.[27] Bauman draws upon Jewish philosopher Emmanuel Levinas to develop an understanding of 'moral acts [that] are intrinsically *free choices*'.[28] These free choices are a response to the face of 'the Other [who] commands us to care by his [sic] *weakness*, not by his *power*'.[29] This 'command', of course, is not an order, literally understood; rather, the face of the other presents a moral responsibility, which one could accept or ignore. This new age, then, need not be a denizen of self-interest, but could spell a beginning of a new social being; not enforceable by law and institution, which belong to the solid order, but a vulnerable and freely chosen being-for-other. That is, at least, the hope of Zygmunt Bauman.

Postmodern?

While justice cannot be done to these writers in a few paragraphs, I hope this outline has been helpful in introducing those who have been most influential on the way in which I understand the postmodern condition. Put very simply, I agree with Lyotard to a point, that postmodernism is a condition of being exhausted by the many universal claims to truth that surround humanity, believing that none of them can support the weight of their own claims. It is to say that the world is so much more complicated, and its systems more contested, than its bureau-crats would care to admit.

The combination of a philosophy that questions everything and a sociology that wants to consume everything has the potential, as Bauman has aptly pointed out, to be either deeply eman-cipatory or profoundly destructive. The question for this book is not to evaluate the postmodern condition, but to ask whether one can map where, in relation to it, the church currently sits. I hope that by taking in a breadth of opinion I will be able to appreciate the different positions – and their differences and similarities – and that options for a way forward may emerge. I also hope to define, and better understand, the emerging church movement, which has become a focus for discussions around the church and the postmodern condition. The next chapter will review the way the emerging church movement has been explained by other writers, highlighting strengths and weaknesses of these narratives, as well as the complexities and diversities that I believe have often been obscured by the hyperbole and politics of some of those involved.

2

Marmite for the church: the loving and loathing of the emerging church

———•••———

In researching the church and the postmodern condition for the past eight years, one of the things that has come across to me very clearly is that people care a great deal about the emerging church movement. Often those writing about it are doing so in order to explain to their audience what they consider to be the greatest opportunity or threat to the church for quite some time. There is a perception that if the movement can be shown in its true colours, then the church will be able to make a wise decision about its future.

This over-politicization of the emerging church is what I feel is causing problems in much of the current research. Not only are the conclusions skewed in one particular direction, but also certain groups are often ignored in order to emphasize a particular character trait of the movement. I believe the emerging church is actually a far less cohesive movement than some of the presentations have suggested, and I intend to provide a way of modelling those observable groups and events that are in conflict with one another. To put the problem in less general terms: how can one best understand what is going on when conservatives and liberals, Catholics and Protestants all make up various aspects of the emerging church movement? As I shall demonstrate, some writers believe the emerging church to be a movement away from formal denominations. This view, though, ignores the many groups, for example Fresh Expressions, that remain in such institutions. Some argue that it is simply a surrendering to the postmodern world, but this takes no note of the criticisms these churches often make of contemporary society. Other writers, however, have recognized that such simplistic definitions will not do when trying to describe the emerging church movement. It is upon their work that I will seek to build up a way of describing not only the emerging church movement, but also the relationship between the church and the postmodern condition.

Eddie Gibbs and Ryan Bolger, Emerging Churches: Creating Christian Communities in Postmodern Cultures

Gibbs and Bolger were the first to offer a book presenting a large, international study of the movement. Through interviewing 50 leaders from the UK and USA, they hoped to be able to define and characterize the churches involved. In the five years they spent on this project, they met with some of the most influential and engaging protagonists from each nation. Almost seven years after its first appearance, it is still seen as one of the most authoritative works in the defining of the 'emerging church'.

In their interviewing of a large sample of leaders from emerging church groups in the UK and USA, Gibbs and Bolger attempt to ascertain the main practices that these groups hold in common.[1] They list nine practices that they believe define the emerging church, three of which – identifying with Jesus, transforming secular space and living as community – are understood to be core to emerging church identity. The other six are shared between the churches and are not always present in their entirety: welcoming the stranger, serving with generosity, participating as producers, creating as created beings, leading as a body, and merging ancient and contemporary spiritualities. These findings appear to have been of help to those in the movement who are trying to understand what the different churches hold in common and what it is they might be hoping to achieve.

The key insight that Gibbs and Bolger outline is that of 'participation', as it is certainly a feature that runs through the churches claiming to be involved in the emerging church movement. From personal discipleship to planning worship, from increasing the sense of community within a church to being involved in social life in local neighbourhoods, the concept of participation is key to understanding these churches. My own meetings with church leaders would echo the kind of talk that Gibbs and Bolger identified: participation is the dominant motif in the way these churches understand themselves. From the moment a person comes across their website or gathering, these churches are keen to offer ways to participate as fully as possible in their communal and worshipping life.

Gibbs and Bolger believe that these nine criteria demonstrate not only the importance of participation, but also the fact that emerging churches are best characterized as communities in which the theology and practices associated with conservative evangelicalism are being broadened. For Gibbs and Bolger, the emerging church offers an antidote to 'modernist' churches that have supposedly privatized and commodified faith.[2] While this is certainly true of some of the churches involved in the emerging church movement, it is not true of them all. The conclusion made by Gibbs and Bolger demonstrates three problems that run throughout their work. First, emerging churches are categorized in too neat a manner, belying the complexity and difference inherent within these different groups. While Gibbs and Bolger attempt to provide for this diversity by listing core and secondary practices, I find the specific practices to be overly general, while the list as a whole is too narrow. Second, there seems to be some confusion in defining emerging churches as 'new' churches that do not belong to another church.[3] This statement seems categorically misinformed, and one need only reference the Fresh Expressions groups (who are part of the Church of England or Methodist Church of Great Britain) to demonstrate that. Further, participant groups such as 'Grace' not only consider themselves part of the Church of England, but also specifically understand themselves as a congregation of a parish church.[4] This definition is also unable to take account of churches whose form is less experimental and which use mainstream liturgical practices, yet share the participative values outlined in their study.

My final concern is that Gibbs and Bolger seem to put too much emphasis on the emerging church understanding itself as a replacement of 'older' forms of church.[5] While this is certainly true in some aspects of the movement (as it is with all church movements), I am unconvinced that it is representative of the whole emerging church movement. Gibbs and Bolger do little to persuade me otherwise, as they do not actually present any evidence to suggest this to be as characteristic of the movement as they claim. I think it is highly problematic to suggest that modernism and its churches are problems to be solved by the 'kingdom of God paradigm' of the emerging church.[6]

While I do believe that the replacement ideology skews the view they are presenting of the emerging church movement, and the authors' focus upon evangelicalism inhibits any discussion about the breadth of the movement, this book remains an important study. It was the first of its kind to recognize and attempt to quantify the way certain churches were engaging with the postmodern condition. Gibbs and Bolger also rightly identified the concept of participation as a way of characterizing the ethos and practices of these churches.

Donald Carson, Becoming Conversant with the Emerging Church: Understanding a Movement and Its Implications

At those times when culture is changing at an alarming rate, it is reassuring to pick up a book that does exactly what you expect it to do. Carson, who is a conservative evangelical theologian, has very helpfully repackaged and updated his *The Gagging of God* in a smaller book with reference to the emerging church movement. The book simply explains how Carson views the emerging church, coming out of a concern that the movement's apparent insistence on church reform appears, to him, to be based upon a poor understanding of modernism and postmodernism.[7]

While he does not engage in interviewing any leaders or meeting with any groups, he has certainly read enough of the book- and web-based literature to see some characteristics that are missed by Gibbs and Bolger. Carson recognizes that this is a diverse movement[8] that is wrestling with profoundly important and difficult questions,[9] and is marked by a sense of protest, particularly towards conservative evangelicalism.[10] He also comments that the literature of the movement tends to oversimplify the questions with which it is wrestling, particularly with regard to modernism, postmodernism and evangelicalism.[11] As a book that appears to have been written as much for evangelicals as it is for the emerging church, it was good to see Carson attempt to suggest what the former might learn from the latter. While this felt rather forced in some parts of his chapter 2, it appeared genuine for Carson to mention how some evangelical Christians would do well to recognize their own cultural situatedness, rather than imagining that they are somehow removed from it.[12]

Carson has a rather confrontational style, and one feels the strength of this as he begins to outline what he believes to be the weaknesses of the emerging church. For Carson, the literature presents a movement that is 'historically skewed and ethically ungrateful' to the traditions from which it is emerging, and 'theologically shallow and intellectually incoherent'.[13] This criticism is centred on five concerns. First, that the movement cannot handle truth, as it presents a false dichotomy between either knowing everything or knowing nothing at all. Carson is keen to suggest that just because one cannot know everything does not mean that one cannot know in an objective and propositional sense.[14] Second, that it appeals to 'tradition' in a rather nebulous and superficial sense, cherry-picking certain practices for aesthetic reasons without fully understanding their theological claims and pedigree.[15] Related to this is his third complaint, that the emerging church does not allow its uses of tradition to be 'controlled by Scripture'.[16]

The next 'failure' to be listed is that there is confusion within the movement around what it means to belong or become, and that the emerging church appears to ignore the fact that the Bible understands Christians to constitute 'a new and distinctive community'.[17] Finally, Carson believes that the emerging church irresponsibly distorts both the Bible and history in order to serve its own ends.[18] He details this final point through an in-depth examination of two books that he feels represent the movement: Brian McLaren's *Generous Orthodoxy* and Steve Chalke's *The Lost Message of Jesus*. Of particular help in this chapter is Carson's demonstration of the superficial way he believes McLaren creates a tapestry of different understandings of Christ in an attempt to explain his position, which encompasses Roman Catholicism, fundamentalism, liberalism and so on. Carson completes his narrative of the emerging church by insisting that the movement represented by these writers' books 'degod[s] God'[19] and has 'largely abandoned the gospel'.[20]

The use of these writers to demonstrate his final point helpfully sums up some of the issues that run through Carson's book. While McLaren is certainly very popular and influential, and Chalke less so, it is unrealistic to expect these two books to be able to represent the whole movement. This is particularly so, given Carson's own admission that it is such a diverse movement.[21] While Carson begins with some accuracy in recognizing elements of the movement, the principal focus upon McLaren prevents Carson's criticisms from being made relevant to the wider emerging church. His method has seriously limited the claims he is able to make, and while he may or may not be correct, he does not provide the evidence to support his claim that it is the emerging church, and not just McLaren, that is skewed, ungrateful, shallow and incoherent.

Further, if these books lack intellectual rigour and depth, it is not necessarily the fault of the ideas within the emerging church, but of the authors of the works themselves. Carson is simply expecting too much from these books and should really have turned to the likes of John Caputo or N. T. Wright, whose ideas fill their pages, if he wished to engage with a greater level of intellectual coherence. Rather than focusing on his issues with McLaren and Chalke, I believe it would have been far more beneficial for Carson to investigate and critique the weight given to these particular books in forming the spoken theology of churches within the movement. The use of populist writing in forming church policies, however, is a criticism that could be made of a vast number of contemporary churches in all kinds of denominations and traditions, and is certainly not unique to the emerging church movement.

If one is able to acknowledge that rather serious issue with method, then *Becoming Conversant with the Emerging Church* has one final and important point to make. The basic premise of the book is that, because it denies objective truth revealed in Scripture,[22] doesn't believe in penal substitution,[23] and doesn't ground its understanding of experience in the truth of the Bible,[24] whatever the emerging church may be, it is not evangelical. For Carson, Christians are known by holding to right doctrine,[25] which is quite different from the openness often observed in the emerging church movement. In this sense, Carson suggests that, whatever may characterize this movement, it is not simply another form of pragmatic evangelicalism that is attempting to be attractive to a new generation. There are simply too many theological differences. Whether some emerging churches consider themselves evangelical or not, they are not concerned with the same things that concern classical evangelicalism: doctrine is presented as dialogue rather than system, the Bible is one among a number of theological resources and the church is characterized by the open participation of all who are present, not by every-member ministry. While Carson's view of evangelicalism may well be rather limited, and his method doesn't reveal a great deal about the emerging church movement, his criticisms question whether this movement is simply just liberal Protestantism under another name.

Tom Sine, The New Conspirators: Creating the Future One Mustard Seed at a Time

Tom Sine's narrating of the movement of churches to engage within the postmodern condition is rather different from that of the other authors outlined in this chapter, and that alone makes his book worth the read. Naming its proponents 'the new conspirators', he divides the movement into four streams, only one of which is labelled 'emerging'. Sine suggests that this movement is characterized by its leaders, who are largely 'young', and 'carefully read the cultural context of a particular community [in order to] create a setting . . . to engage individuals in the surrounding community'.[26]

The four streams are: emerging, missional, mosaic and monastic. The emerging stream is characterized by an understanding of the gospel as narrative rather than in propositional terms, works creatively with word, image, the sacred and the 'profane', calls for a whole-life faith, is outward-focused and views mission in a holistic manner. The organization of the groups is also characterized by their non-hierarchical structures, which attempt to reduce, as much as possible, the level of bureaucracy that Sine believes has become endemic in many American churches.[27] Later in the book he also acknowledges the importance of experiential participation within these groups.[28] Sine also offers a criticism of this stream, stating that while it is highly creative, such imagination tends to be restricted within 'the box called "worship"'.[29]

The missional stream tends to be led by seminary-trained leaders and seeks renewal within traditional denominations. This stream also calls for a new commitment to mission, both global and local.[30] The mosaic stream is made up of intentionally multicultural groups, in which the different cultures present are encouraged to shape the local church directly. As with the missional stream, these groups are also extremely focused upon local and global mission.[31] The final stream, monastic, tends to have no interest in church planting, but rather focuses upon deepening spiritual practices, and residential communities tend to live or work among the poor.[32]

The remainder of the book is concerned with what these groups are, or should be, doing in relating to the postmodern condition. Sine sees the world as a conflict of big projects, largely between the false promises of consumerism and the true hope of the kingdom of God. He explains that globalization

has changed the world and taken the form of an empire, forcing
people to live under its free-market values.[33] Within this story,
Sine suggests, there is room for belief in, even worship of, God,
so long as such faith is not taken too seriously; the true Lord
is 'the global free market, political and economic power, and
random mutations of nature – period.'[34] This story has been
told by the storytellers of the 'global mall', and Sine suggests
that Christians have trusted this to such an extent that it has
begun 'to eclipse the ancient story and the future hope' of
Christian faith.[35] The result is the haemorrhaging of the contemporary church;[36] the hope, however, lies in the re-imagining
of the new conspirators.[37]

The re-imagining that characterizes all four streams of the
movement is thought to be grounded in the work of N. T. Wright,
as well as the theologian Stanley Hauerwas[38] and the missiolo-
gist Stuart Murray.[39] Through these writers, the leaders have
learned to trust not only that there is a scriptural grand narrative that can be known, but also that the role of the church is
to improvise faithfully the story in the contemporary world.[40]
For Sine, one of the most important ways in which the new
conspirators can faithfully improvise is by making more time
for charity by spending less time at work.[41] Not only does this
meet the needs of the poor and marginalized, not only is this
a response to the call of the gospel, but it also tells the Christian
story by placing God and his people before money and power.

The most important offering this book has to make, in my
view at least, is in the author's attempt to broaden the definition
of 'emerging church'. Sine appears to recognize the diversity
of those who have been associated with the emerging church
movement, and so resists offering a simple definition. Rather,
he writes about new and traditional churches that are joining
in 'this conspiracy of creativity' that is challenging the story of
the global mall.[42] The model of the four 'streams' is extremely

helpful in moving the discussion away from the narrow 'emerging church' label that tends to dominate the discussion of churches of this kind.

That said, I am not sure that Sine goes far enough in broadening the definition of these 'new conspirators'. For example, while Sine is correct in discussing the central role played by the works of N. T. Wright within some aspects of this movement, it is less obvious in others, some of whom would disagree with Wright on many points. Further, while some churches within this movement share Sine's disdain for free-market capitalism, others do not, which suggests that Sine's defining is still too narrow, and the categories require further work.

Andrew Davison and Alison Milbank, For the Parish: A Critique of Fresh Expressions

In 2004 the Church of England published a report, *Mission-Shaped Church*, calling for new structures to sit alongside its historic parochial structures, which cover the whole of England. This led to the creation (in partnership with the Methodist Church of Great Britain) of 'Fresh Expressions', a movement whose leaders have been licensed by bishops to work within areas that already have a parish church. From Autumn 2012 the leaders of these groups, who have come to be known as 'pioneer ministers', began to receive specialized training that is supposed to be quite different from the training received by other Anglican ordinands. All this in less than a decade? While appearing slow to those in corporate training and development, this is the Church of England in hyperdrive; and it makes Davison and Milbank decidedly nervous.

Though they do not offer an analysis of specific churches, Davison and Milbank present a largely negative storying of the UK Fresh Expressions movement. There is a clear disdain for its organization, which is an attitude that can come across as patronizing and sometimes childish,[43] and the analysis often depends upon caricatures of the movement rather than actual examples. For this reason, the book has received a divided response within the UK. Despite the authors' rather shrill tone and headline-grabbing hyperbole, however, it has a great deal to offer.

For the Parish functions as an excellent case study measuring the impact that the movement of churches to engage within postmodern cultures is having upon a traditional denomination, in this case, the Church of England. The subject of the book demonstrates my concern that Gibbs' and Bolger's definition of 'emerging church' (as something that is new) is a case of misunderstanding and simplification. The book is also helpful in the way it discusses the theological and philosophical issues that are at stake within the discussions about the church and the postmodern condition.

While *For the Parish* is presented as a critique of Fresh Expressions, it is really an engagement with *Mission-Shaped Church* and the vision that report appears to convey. One of the central concerns raised by Davison and Milbank is the way the report believes that one can change the practices of the church without altering its nature.[44] One hardly needs to adopt the same position as Davison and Milbank in order to see the importance of this question, which has still not been fully explored. To what extent does the changing of what the church does, and is seen to do, change not only people's perception of it, but also the church's very nature? Davison and Milbank carefully explore specific examples of this issue, most helpfully under the themes of cultural accommodation and the misunderstanding of tradition.

Quite simply, the authors find contemporary society to be largely 'vacuous, selfish and lost',[45] so that any dialogue and accommodation runs counter to the gospel of the church. The authors cite the work of Pete Ward as exemplifying this 'merging' into postmodernity. The basic premise of Ward's *Liquid Church* follows the work of Zygmunt Bauman, which I outlined in Chapter 1. 'Liquid church' lies in the movement of culture from solid, hierarchical societies to a liquid consumerism in which people are free to construct their identities through the purchasing of signs and symbols.[46] Ward views these socio-cultural moves as neutral, being no different from any other cultural change in the history of the world, and so encourages the church to go through the same transition.[47] His hope is that, in changing the language and practices of the church to fit with this liquid modernity, it will not lose its relevance in the world.[48] Davison and Milbank believe the opposite should be the case: the church should be a distinctive body of resistance, rather than attempting to close the gap between the church and culture.[49] This is similar to the criticism made by Martyn Percy, who believes that Fresh Expressions is a form of collusion with consumerism and post-institutionalism.[50] For Davison and Milbank, the response of the church to postmodern cultures should be 'strong, confident and poised, arising from a community that is formed by Christian, rather than secular, values'.[51]

Davison and Milbank also suggest that *Mission-Shaped Church* is obsessed with choice and novelty in such a way that it apes consumerist culture. They argue that, as well as being another example of cultural accommodation, this consumerism has come at the cost of the traditions that have been handed down through the church. The authors are highly critical of the idea that Fresh Expressions might shed the historical embodiment of the church for the sake of mission, asking whether such an idea even makes sense.[52]

The question that arises out of these criticisms regarding cultural accommodation is a vital one for churches which claim to minister within postmodern cultures. By fusing ancient liturgies with secular music, not citing the creeds, and meeting on Wednesdays rather than Sundays, has secularism actually become more dominant within the church than these groups realize? Had Davison and Milbank actually taken the time to study some of the Fresh Expressions groups, they might well have been able to present an answer to this vital question. Rather, they offer a very clear answer of their own: a church is either compromised and accommodating towards secularism (as with Fresh Expressions), or it is resistant, and so a place in which salvation can be found. There are some problems here, and I can't help but think they begin with the purpose of the book. *For the Parish* was not written as a critique of Fresh Expressions groups, otherwise it would have contained a section in which leaders or congregations were interviewed or observed. I'm not even convinced that it was written with the primary intention of critiquing *Mission-Shaped Church*, although that is certainly an important and welcome part of the book. Rather, I believe this is an attempt to popularize the particular movement to which Davison and Milbank both belong, that is, radical orthodoxy. All of the works that belong to this movement have been highly erudite displays of great theological rigour, and there has certainly been a need to present the views of the movement at a more popular level, which this book appears to do extremely well.

Without going into too much detail, I would describe radical orthodoxy as a movement that rejects, as secular and godless, the liberal Christianity that was popular at the end of the last century. Instead, radical orthodoxy insists that theology must become the main way of understanding the world; science, philosophy and language can only be understood within a particular theological framework. This, its leaders claim, is the only way to reassert doctrinal truth in opposition to secularism and postmodern despair. The doctrine of the Incarnation is central to this framework; just as God-made-flesh is necessary for salvation, so this salvation is inseparable from the place and institution of the church. This leads to the call for a new Christendom as the only way people may be saved from a postmodern, capitalist world.[53]

This book offers a very helpful view of what the church under radical orthodoxy might look like. When a person is baptized, he or she would be welcomed into a new society, which is democratically organized under a holy hierarchy of bishops, priests and deacons.[54] The church would be a distinctive community, set apart from the secular nations, and formed by its liturgy, calendar, spaces and stories. Through living within this community of virtue, individuals learn how secularism has sold them false promises, and so are enabled to see the world as it really is, in the light of God.[55] Building on the work of Stanley Hauerwas, Davison and Milbank state that it is only within the church that one can learn and develop the Christian virtues.[56] While such a vision can appear rather appealing, it contains assumptions that I find somewhat problematic.

First, there is too clear a separation between the supposed accommodation involved in the work of Fresh Expressions, and the resistance of the radical orthodoxy approach. While some, or even all, churches engaging in postmodern dialogues may be as culturally compromised as the book describes, the authors do not have the evidence to make such a claim. It may be the case that these churches are able to engage critically with their cultural situation, so that they are able to occupy a more positive position than that envisioned by radical orthodoxy. This is not to say that Davison and Milbank are necessarily wrong, but that they have not provided enough evidence really to convince us that Fresh Expressions is simply a surrendering to postmodern culture.

In addition to their posture towards culture, the position radical orthodoxy and Fresh Expressions have towards church tradition is also important. Davison and Milbank claim that the inherited church focuses on tradition as given, rather than something one can choose as an option. To illustrate this, Davison and Milbank turn to the way the Creed is recited in a service, explaining that when the congregation reach the section about the Incarnation, the people bow.[57] Their own example actually helps to demonstrate one of the problems with this line of criticism, as such a practice is a tradition that is far from universal within the Church of England. In this sense, it demonstrates the nature of tradition within the Church of England as opposed to other churches: this tradition is plural and – within limits set by canon law, bishops and synods, formularies and creeds – is something with which an individual, parish, diocese and province enter into dialogue. If the understanding of tradition were a uniform given, as is suggested by the authors, then there would be far less diversity within the Church of England than currently exists. On this point, it can be said that radical orthodoxy appears to be at odds with the ecclesiology of the Church of England.

I do wonder whether radical orthodoxy, as presented by Davison and Milbank, is really as different from some emerging church groups as they claim. For all of their posturing against the latter movement, they do share some striking similarities. Many emerging churches are interested in continuing and renewing the ancient traditions of the church as a response to postmodern culture, and not necessarily in a superficial manner. Also, many claim to have entered into positive, but not uncritical, dialogues with postmodern philosophy, and a significant number also share Davison's and Milbank's disdain of late-capitalist society, believing that the church should stand in protest against such nihilistic consumerism. It could be argued that there is enough commonality to warrant a careful look at radical orthodoxy as an element within the emerging church movement, rather than as a move against it.

The reason for my rather lengthy engagement with Davison and Milbank is that the criticisms they make about churches engaging in postmodern cultures are important and deserve to be taken seriously. The relationships between these churches and the church catholic, between form and content, between the church and broad cultural movements, between the churches of the present and the past, are issues that have not been taken seriously enough by other commentators. However, the presentation in this work is intended to suggest that a church has either folded into the 'nihilistic swamp' of postmodernity,[58] or been faithful to Christ in the manner of radical orthodoxy. Through a careful analysis of the participant churches, I would like to question whether this is really the case, as well as investigating whether Davison and Milbank have more in common with the emerging church movement than they realize.

Scot McKnight, Peter Rollins, Kevin Corcoran, Jason Clark, Church in the Present Tense: A Candid Look at What's Emerging

This series of essays is written by four major protagonists within the emerging church movement, offering their own narratives of what they believe is going on. While there are no specific interviews or group observations, the views are based on their many years of involvement with the churches and groups that make up this movement. While this leads to a slight confusion as to whether they are writing about what they see in the movement, or what they hope it might become, there are still some helpful comments that are worth considering.

Corcoran's introduction is very helpful, setting out his understanding of the evolution of the movement in the UK and USA. According to his narrative, the emerging church began within the alternative worship movement in the UK, and largely within the Church of England.[59] This is why, he argues, the emerging church in the UK tends to be more focused upon worship than it is upon other elements of church life.[60] In the USA, however, Corcoran explains that the emerging church began as a reaction against evangelical Protestantism, which has caused the groups to have a greater focus upon 're-imagining' theology as well as its practices.[61] What unites the movement in both nations, as well as in other nations, is a sensitivity to the postmodern condition, humility around what a person can know (epistemology), suspicion towards 'tidy theological boxes', and what constitutes being in or out, either of the church or of salvation. He also observes that there is a tendency towards the use of hyperbole that, while possibly unhelpful, is intended to wake the church from its 'dogmatic slumber'.[62]

Corcoran also observes that emerging church groups tend to have a concern for the present (hence the book's title), which can be seen in four aspects common to the whole movement: community, transformation, worship and social engagement.[63] While the second and fourth values seemed to be rather similar, the narrative being presented is of groups who are highly committed to, and intentional about, their life together in a non-hierarchical manner. They are politically active from a liberal and left perspective, and would view anyone doing such work as engaging in the work of God, regardless of his or her creed. Finally, their worship tends to be highly 'tactile', a word that describes the creative and participatory mode of their meetings far better than the usual (and misused) term, 'sacramental'.[64] Certainly the description of these groups as politically left, understanding themselves to be creating a space that has the potential to be an alternative to free-market capitalism, runs through the various essays in the book.[65]

Church in the Present Tense demonstrates, contrary to some of Davison's and Milbank's criticisms, that thinking within the emerging church movement can be far from superficial. The authors offer a great deal of insight into the intentions and concerns of some of the groups within this movement. While Corcoran affirms the way these groups attempt to express their beliefs with a sense of humility, he is concerned that talk of 'mystery' has become so commonplace that it has become a way of avoiding difficult questions of truth: it is easier to say something is a mystery than attempt to explain it. His way beyond this is to follow Stanley Hauerwas's approach and see the world as a conflict of big projects based on particular big stories. While free-market capitalism offers a story of consumerism and self-interest, the church is called to stand as a community of aliens among this, inviting others to join in their protest against the violence of the nations and the market, and to learn the virtues of Christ in his church.[66]

In his essays, Rollins is equally critical of contemporary capitalism and suggests the church can and should be an alternative community, but without the boundaries that are inherent in Hauerwas's approach. Here, Rollins offers the image not of an emerging church or emerging conversation, but of emerging cohorts:[67] artists on the margins of the church and society, creating transformative art. The beliefs, practices and architecture of the church allow people to feel as though they are doing something of note, so that they can carry on their day jobs and continue to support the dominance of free-market capitalism. (I will explore Rollins's ideas in greater detail in

Chapter 4.) The emerging cohorts are the ones who have broken out of organized religion; free of such institutional domination, they create spaces in pubs and cafés that make it easier, even inevitable, for people to have honest conversations that might help them begin to imagine a more radical view of the world.[68]

The view offered by this book ably highlights some of the problems with Davison and Milbank's caricature of the emerging church movement. It demonstrates not only the depth of thinking within some of these groups, but also the fact that they cannot simply be stereotyped as churches that have surrendered to postmodern criticism. While Davison and Milbank are correct to critique the theology of Pete Ward on this front, as he certainly does advocate a consumerist theology, this book presents emerging churches as existing in conflict with the story and values of free-market capitalism. As with Sine's book, then, the most helpful narrating to emerge from this work is the way it broadens the definition of what an emerging church might be. Put alongside the work of Pete Ward, emerging churches appear to exist along a spectrum ranging from Ward's pragmatic approach of re-plotting theology along consumerist principles, to the separatist neo-Christendom of radical orthodoxy, whereby the church exists outside of the market and in opposition to the nations. In addition, the presence of Rollins within the same movement as Anglican Fresh Expressions suggests a second continuum, in this case between those who exist within an institution, and those who hope for the destruction of such institutions. It will be helpful to ask whether these, and other, spectrums can be observed across the participant churches of this study, in what way they are made manifest, and whether they provide a helpful way of defining what is meant by 'emerging church'.

Mary Gray-Reeves and Michael Perham, The Hospitality of God: Emerging Worship for a Missional Church

While not being completely uncritical of their participants, the main thrust of this book is to ask what the inherited church might learn from the worship of the emerging church movement within Anglicanism. Gray-Reeves and Perham, both Anglican bishops, attempt to focus their research upon emerging church groups from within US and UK Anglicanism. They do not study groups from non-Anglican evangelicalism, nor do they wish to research into older Anglican churches, but rather focus on Anglican churches that are intentionally inclusive, holding the Eucharist and liturgy as central to their life together.[69] That said, the authors clearly struggle to keep within these boundaries, citing one participant church that celebrates the Eucharist only once every four months, and another two churches that would not describe themselves as part of the emerging church movement. As the authors admit, they had to move beyond their own description of the emerging church within Anglicanism because of 'powerful experiences . . . within the inherited church'.[70] Through focusing upon worship, they believe they have been able to attend to issues of community, authority and accountability.[71]

The overall narrative being offered by Gray-Reeves and Perham is that the mission of these emerging churches is to connect with those who have been disenfranchised by various institutions and the church, while also changing the institutional church itself. This is explored in four themes that run throughout the book, the first of which is their low view of hierarchy. The authors claim that these Anglican emergent churches are distrustful of hierarchy and see language that attempts to discuss

34

distinctive, liturgical roles as unhelpful. For example, while all of the groups had a single person who presided over the Eucharist, the role was inhabited in a low-key manner and alongside a great deal of lay participation.[72] They also suggest that any leadership or decision-making that takes place within a local church has about it an 'indigenous authenticity'.[73] This, however, strikes one as a rather grand way of saying that these churches have a congregational approach to local church organization, albeit with a completely open decision-making body. What was intriguing, and unfortunately not more deeply explored, was the positive way the leaders spoke of their relationship with their bishop:[74] one wonders how this was viewed by the rest of the participant church, and also about the extent to which the bishop was involved in the practices that were contrary to canon law. For instance, local autonomy and personal authenticity were seen as so important that most of these churches were reported to be uncomfortable about saying the Creed, not wanting to give assent to something that was not a personally held belief.[75]

The second theme is the high expectation the leaders and congregation had of the participation of local people within the organization of the worship and liturgy. The authors observe that the planning of the group meetings was so important to the understanding of discipleship that 'there [was] almost more interest in sharing in the devising of the liturgy than having a role within its celebration.'[76] While much of what was experienced in these churches shared an Anglican 'shape' to their worship, the words created by these groups were often local and original works of liturgy, albeit unauthorized. Similarly, the churches often had musicians who were able to compose original pieces for specific services of worship. The authors felt that, as with the low view of hierarchy, the high expectation of participation arose organically from the churches' commitment to hospitality. Such was the strength of this inclusivity that the

churches would again break canon law by, for example, allowing anyone, regardless of their faith or sacramental standing,
to receive Holy Communion,[77] or, in two of the churches,
having lay people presiding at the Eucharist.[78] While the first
of these examples is more commonplace in the USA, it remains
contrary to canon law in the Church of England. The second
example runs contrary to canon law throughout all provinces
of the Anglican Communion, as it directly challenges the understanding of priesthood held by the Anglican, Orthodox and
Roman Catholic Churches. As with their view of hierarchy, such
levels of participation gave people a great sense of belonging
to the local church, but often caused the churches to have little
sense of how they might belong to the church catholic in any
specific way.[79]

The third observation, which the authors return to on a
number of occasions, is the inherent diversity within these
churches. Even though the participant churches tended to be
socially liberal and inclusive, with a strong desire to engage in
contemporary culture,[80] Gray-Reeves and Perham observed that
the political views were too broad to be a unifying factor in
these churches.[81] They suggest that it was the way in which the
Eucharist was celebrated, without any concern for a common
understanding of what was happening, that enabled cohesion.[82]
The authors believe this is such a positive and appropriate
manner of celebration that the wider church should be challenged
by its inherent inclusivity. Such a challenge is said to offer a
serious critique of the inherited church's exclusivity in insisting
on a particular sacramental position (i.e. being baptized and
confirmed) before being able to receive Holy Communion.[83]
In addition to this, Gray-Reeves and Perham also suggest – and
one senses that the authors themselves were surprised by this –
that liturgical complexity appears to be helpful in sustaining
a diverse church. Contrary to modern liturgical renewal, which

insists upon simplifying liturgical action so as not to confuse the congregation, the participant churches suggest that complexity provides a multilayered liturgy that involves different people in different ways, and is thus able to hold together a congregation with greater diversity.[84]

The final recurring theme is that of 'belonging, behaving, believing'. According to the authors, the change in culture means that the once-expected linear progression from baptism to confirmation, and on into sacramental church life until one's funeral, is no longer prevalent. It is argued that, while the emerging church understands this, '[i]n the traditional church the linear path to faith still dominates.'[85] In response to this, the emerging church is said to have reversed the traditional church's order, so that one belongs before behaving and believing.[86] While this is rather familiar ground to anyone who has been involved in researching the emerging church movement, it is worth noting that the authors hope the inherited church would also learn to see this order as being a much more muddled process rather than a straightforward progression.[87] The problem, for me at least, is not that I disagree with the authors, but that I believe many institutional churches already hold to a more nuanced understanding of faith development. While churches may well place a priority upon one of those values at the expense of the other two, it would be rare, certainly within the US and UK Anglican Church, to see a linear understanding of Christian discipleship. This theme feels like an unfair caricature of the inherited church; while I accept that the Eucharist is usually withheld within the Church of England until a person is baptized and (usually) confirmed, that is not evidence enough of the linear and rigid understanding of Christian discipleship suggested by Gray-Reeves and Perham. It may be more accurate to suggest that such practices in the inherited church are at odds with much of its thinking.

Through their low view of hierarchy, high view of equal participation, holding of diversity, and placing less emphasis upon believing before belonging, Gray-Reeves and Perham present a vivid and convincing picture of the emerging church movement within Anglicanism. There is a sense that the leaders of these churches are intentionally reaching out to connect with those whose exposure to continued institutional failure has led to their being disenfranchised from institutions (including, but not exclusively, the church), so that they might be enabled to configure life (and therefore faith) in this new setting.[88] This desire does not appear to come from the leaders' need to get others to copy their own configuration; rather they wish to help create churches in which the resources of the church may be opened up to all. This appears to match with my own research, and is a helpful way to define those of the emerging church movement who wish to stay within specific denominations.

Given that both of the authors are bishops, however, I am disappointed that there is not more depth to the discussion about the relationship these Anglican churches have with their own bishops and dioceses, as well as neighbouring parishes. The fact that certain aspects of canon law are not taken seriously is far from being the subject of an insular debate, but acts as a case study for how those disenfranchised by what they perceive as institutional failure might continue to relate to public and private institutions. A deeper discussion would have further strengthened this already-helpful study of institutional Christianity and the postmodern condition.

Criticizing the emerging church movement is not a particular feature of this book. While Gray-Reeves and Perham are far from sycophantic towards the movement, the hope that these churches will renew the institutional churches shapes the outcomes more than I believe to be helpful; a problem that becomes particularly apparent in their chapter 8. Here the authors claim that the emerging church movement is concerned with those seeking to be 'fed' and with the wider community, whereas institutional churches 'are primarily concerned with their own survival, and only secondarily with the spiritually hungry, or those otherwise in need'.[89] This is a profoundly unhelpful statement that unnecessarily pits the emerging church movement against the institution of the church. Furthermore, this is simply untrue, and is proven as such in Gray-Reeves and Perham's own research: both St Mark's Cathedral and St Paul's Church in Seattle, key participants in this research, are traditional Anglican churches that do not define themselves as part of the emerging church movement. Rather than being exceptions to the rule, could it be that these churches demonstrate that 'emerging churches' have been too narrowly defined by the authors? Is it possible that, just as Sine's and Corcoran's works have broadened the definition of groups that might be considered as part of the same movement, 'traditional churches' are also involved? If this is the case, and I shall attempt to look at it within this project, then terms such as 'emerging' and 'traditional' are brought under serious scrutiny.

Doug Gay, Remixing the Church: Towards an Emerging Ecclesiology

The final book in my discussion is included because it helps to illustrate the problems inherent in writing about a movement such as the emerging church. Having been heavily involved in the movement within the UK, Gay is well placed to offer commentary, narrative and definition. However, the method employed prevents this book from being all it should be, causing a one-sided definition and a retrograde move in the study of this movement.

The framework holding the book together is Gay's metaphor that the emerging church is characterized by a series of movements that form a never-ending spiral. Inherent to the emerging church is its 'auditing', which is explained as a commitment to always seeking reformation.[90] This flows into a 'retrieval', through which churches and groups explore the 'deep/catholic dimension of their own ecclesial identities'.[91] Having begun to use practices from different traditions, the emerging church 'unbundles' them from their original theological context, and seeks a different way of understanding the theology that these practices embody and convey.[92] In addition to this engagement with other traditions, the emerging church is also known by its 'supplementing', by which Gay means innovating something that had not previously existed within the church.[93] The end result of these four movements is to propel the emerging church to 'remix' all that has emerged into a new way of being church,[94] which will ultimately be reformed, leading to the start of a new part of the spiral. While I find the metaphor and terms rather confusing, it seems that the implicit point being made is that this is the journey the church has always been on. What we currently know as the emerging church is simply the latest instalment in the continual reformation of the church.

If such a conclusion sounds rather similar to a Reformed, Protestant view of the church, then that appears to be entirely deliberate, as Gay's 'working assumption' is that the emerging church movement is 'decisively located within low church Protestantism'.[95] This book presents an emerging church that is Protestant, but also takes practices from older traditions without any commitment to their context (whether theological, ecclesiological or historical). This is a post-denominational ecclesiology (which, unlike Gay, I would argue is different from ecumenical) that has arisen out of Gay's own Protestant thinking and experience. Any ecclesial institutional presence in the emerging church is either out of necessity (groups may be linked to a denomination, but Gay has 'heard many people say . . . "I see myself as more post-denominational"'),[96] or a desire for the powers to control what is going on.[97]

According to Gay, the emerging church is 'an irreverent new wave of grassroots ecumenism, propelled from within low church Protestantism by a mix of longing, curiosity and discontent'. It cares not for institutional protocols, being engendered by 'innovation and experimentation . . . in response to the Spirit's prompting'.[98] This presentation of the emerging church as a Protestant stand against the outdated and 'theologically baffling'[99] institutional church may win many fans, but not to the improvement of emerging church research, nor to the development of the emerging church itself. This is little more than a thin veneer of liberal Protestantism on what is a rather illiberal definition of the emerging church. Either one is post-denominational, anti-institutional and low church Protestant (but only in the way Gay understands such concepts), or one cannot be in the emerging church. Gay does not attempt to explain where that leaves those within movements such as Fresh Expressions, 'Presby-mergents', 'Angli-mergents' and such like, and does not entertain the possibility that one might be committed to both the emerging church movement and a particular denomination.

I believe this flawed definition has emerged from a flawed method: if one sets out to reflect only on one's personal experiences in order to define a movement, no matter how experienced one might be of that movement, the work will only ever be based on anecdote, and will simply universalize one's own experiences. Gay has ignored the emerging church studies that have been gradually moving away from tight definitions of an identifiable group, preferring instead to examine overlapping clusters of movements, and has thus repeated the early mistakes of Gibbs and Bolger. Further, contradicting his own desire to 'recover and promote a more collegial spirit',[100] he treats critics of the emerging church movement far too harshly.[101] He rushes in to criticize their tone with such force that he misses what is valuable in their arguments. As I hope to have demonstrated, the works of Carson, Davison and Milbank may at times be frustrating, but they have important and thoughtful comments to make. All theses and movements need to learn from criticism in order to grow, and Gay's own concept of 'unbundling' could have been so much more helpful had he engaged with Davison's and Milbank's genuinely helpful criticisms of the separation of form and content.

Despite the recent attempts to understand the emerging church movements on their own terms, Gay has written a book that feels less like an exercise in definition and more like an imperial naming and claiming. To draw such tight boundaries around a movement as diverse as this would require a great deal of evidence. Gay, however, does not provide any evidence except his own experiences, and simply expects the reader to trust and follow. This will not do, particularly when a casual glance around emerging church groups suggests something far more complex than that of Gay's presentation.

This book does two things that are of importance to this current work, however. First, if one can put aside Gay's universalizing of his own experiences, he opens up a particular part of the emerging church movement, which is helpful when attempting to map out the different groups. Second, he underlines the problems inherent in attempting to offer a single definition: while such a definition may be possible, it will only arise after taking into consideration the diversity of churches and groups involved in this movement.

Moving on

At first, the various narratives on offer may appear confusing: is it correct that the church's relationship with the postmodern condition demonstrates how the church has lost its battle with secularism and consumerism, or does it rather indicate a new space through which a new society might be formed? Is it an anti-institutional movement, a renewal movement or a new form of Christendom? Is it a big project formed by a big story in conflict with other, idolatrous projects, such as capitalism; or is it a complex dialogue of projects and stories from many different traditions? With so many questions, it is forgivable to think that a task of definition is impossible. There may, however, be another way of looking at this plethora of narratives.

I believe that the major cause of this confusion begins with each author having looked at only one corner of a larger movement. It isn't that the authors haven't looked at enough churches in terms of quantity, but that they haven't looked at the whole spectrum of the way the church relates to the postmodern condition. Before attempting to define, narrate or critique the movement, they have selected participant churches or leaders according to their own assumptions of what constitutes an 'emerging church'. This is one of the reasons why the various definitions and narratives contradict one another, as well as being unable to make sense of the breadth across the movement. It is not that the narratives are 'wrong', but that they each offer accounts of parts of a wider movement in which churches are intentionally responding to the postmodern condition. While Sine recognizes this up to a point, he still works within too narrow a framework that excludes older, institutional churches. Also, the method of looking for, and defining, small groups (as he does with emerging, missional, mosaic and monastic) may not be the most appropriate way to understand the whole.

I also think that asking the question, 'What is the emerging church?' is to begin in the wrong place, as it assumes that there is such a thing as 'the emerging church'. If the confusion and conflict of the above narratives suggests anything, it is that such an entity simply does not exist in the way that people have assumed. The 'emerging church' may well be a helpful banner to gather people to discuss the church and the postmodern condition, but the books that I have read do not suggest that the groups involved really have enough coherence to be labelled in a collective way. There is certainly a movement within the church that seeks to engage with the postmodern condition (either positively or negatively), but it is far broader than can be captured in a presentation of the emerging church.

I believe that, in order to understand this whole movement, questions need to be asked of a wide range of churches that claim to minister within the postmodern condition, so that key tensions and poles can be identified. In some ways, extreme reactions can already be seen in the literature that I have presented in this chapter: the new Christendom of radical orthodoxy, Pete Ward's merging of theology into consumerism, and the radical nonconformism of Peter Rollins. What is investigated by this project is whether these ideas are present in the thinking of the various church leaders with whom I have met, so that a map can be drawn of the different ways the church relates to the postmodern condition.

I have met with 25 leaders of different churches in the UK and USA, from as wide a selection as is possible. These interviews were set up by my sending out an identical email to as many groups and leaders as possible. I simply explained that I was interested in the relationship of the church and the postmodern condition, and invited them to meet with me.

While I would have liked to have had a larger sample, I was extremely pleased that the range was almost as broad as is possible. With the significant exceptions of the Eastern Orthodox Churches, I have been able to meet with priests, ministers and lay leaders from Roman Catholic, independent, Methodist, evangelical, Baptist, Quaker, Pentecostal, and Anglican churches. I met each of these leaders at least once, and each meeting was structured around the same questions. I then transcribed each interview, and analysed the language used. The next chapter is intended to give an impression of what those meetings were like, and what ideas emerged in the conversations.

3

Conversations: church leaders discuss the postmodern condition

———————◆•◆———————

Rather than presenting the themes and foci of the various interviews I have conducted, I have decided to demonstrate my findings using the words of six of the participants, which have been organized as a single conversation. While the interviews were conducted separately, each of the participants was answering the same questions and dealing with the same issues, around which this 'conversation' has been organized. This has the advantage of presenting the breadth of views that exist in a clear manner that relies on little of my own interpretation, except that of editing. Of course, such organization carries a level of interpretation. However, I have attempted to do this with as little interference as possible, organizing the answers around the sets of questions the participants were dealing with in the interviews.

In addition to clarity, I hope that this presentation will also display the richness and thoughtfulness that the various participants displayed in the interviews. As I have argued in Chapter 2, it is all too easy to caricature various churches and ministers according to one's own expectations. It is my hope that this chapter will help move discussions around the church and the postmodern condition away from caricature by listening to the beliefs and hopes of those who are ministering and leading in the church today. Before moving on to the conversations, it will be helpful first to introduce each of the participants.

Callid Keefe-Perry is a member of the Religious Society of Friends in Rochester, New York, and has served as a teacher of Quakerism at the Pendle Hill retreat centre for Friends. He is a co-convener of the Rochester Emergent Village Cohort, which is an international network of locally based groups exploring emerging church issues. He has published in the field of 'postmodern theology' and is particularly interested in its association with literature in what he calls 'theo-poetics'.

Sue Wallace is a Church of England team vicar in Leeds Parish Church, UK, where she has a particular responsibility for liturgy, arts and music. Previous to this, she founded and led the two York-based groups, Visions and Transcendence, which are part of the Fresh Expressions movement. She has published books on alternative and multisensory worship.

Winnie Varghese is the priest-in-charge of St Mark's-in-the-Bowery, an Episcopal church near the Lower East Side of New York. The church is well known for its historic and continued participation in the arts, liturgical innovation and civil rights activism. The Sunday services at St Mark's, while being centred on the Eucharist, are highly inventive and participatory. Previous to this role, Winnie was the chaplain of Columbia University, and has written on areas of Christianity and social justice.

Jonny Baker has been a member of Grace almost since it was first conceived as an alternative worship community in West London. He works for the missionary organization Church Mission Society (CMS), in which he leads the newly founded pioneer mission leadership training course. Jonny is an active and popular blogger, and has also published on alternative worship. He is one of the trustees of Greenbelt Christian Arts Festival.

Stephen Gerth is the rector of St Mary's, Times Square in New York. Both Stephen and the church are in the Anglo-Catholic tradition of the Episcopal Church, and place a great deal of emphasis upon liturgy and the sacraments. Owing to its frequent use of incense, St Mary's is often known as 'Smokey Mary's'. The services are formal in nature, mainly led by the celebrant and other attending ordained ministers, and the singing consists of largely non-congregational anthems and chants sung by the choir.

Roy Searle is one of the founders and leaders of the Northumbria Community, a 'new' monastic movement that has its roots in the late 1970s. Companions of the Northumbria Community can be found across the world, living either alone or as part of community. Previous to this, Roy was a minister in two Baptist churches in the north of England, and he has also served as the president of the Baptist Union of Great Britain.

Callid, Sue and Jonny all self-identify as being connected within Fresh Expressions or emerging church groups; Roy identifies as being positively engaged with Fresh Expressions and emerging church groups; Winnie and Stephen do not self-identify as being part of emerging church and Fresh Expressions groups.

There's a great deal of talk about 'postmodernity'; do you see anything in society and culture that suggests this?

Sue: I suppose my first thought on that is that there's no such thing as 'culture' (singular) any more; it's multiple cultures. I suppose it's like a cynical, morphing, shifting, shaping sea of insecurity and lack of certainty – that's how I would define it. But as soon as you think you've grasped it, it morphs into something else.

Roy: Postmodernity to me is the ending of one culture. The origin of the Northumbria Community, actually, was a kind of intuitive sense that we were living through the ending of a culture that had been around for a long time; call it 'modernity', whatever. You can't easily define it because we're not there yet; we're in it, we're emerging into it, but how can you easily quantify something? And perhaps the nature of postmodernity is not to use the criteria of quantification and quantifying things as we have done in modernity, if that doesn't sound too confusing.

Postmodernity speaks to me of diversity and pluralism, and the rejection of the metanarratives, and a kind of absence of a story that coheres and sticks us and glues us together and makes us society. And I think we're in a bit of a crisis in England, but also a great opportunity [because], for me, postmodernity throws us as many opportunities as it does challenges. I think there's a vacuum created by postmodernity that is a great opportunity to live out the gospel. I almost said, 'speak' out the gospel, but I actually think words have become more meaningless in a postmodern context. And yet narrative, I think, is a really quite important thing.

Postmodernity is very confusing, and in England today it's characterized by incessant choosing. I think endless choice is exhausting; endless choice is confusing; endless choice is, I think, more rooted in a consumerist market-driven-ness than it is in true freedom.

I think biblically I would look at postmodernity within the context of exile. I would say that Western culture is in exile, the church is in exile, and with it has come, culturally, a loss of idealism.

Jonny: Consumerism is one of the big themes for me; it's probably just changed in the postmodern world [compared] to the modern world. In that, identity under modernity would be characterized around production. So what you did as a career,

or whatever, was who you are. Whereas I think in the consumer environment we're in, identity's much more constructed
around what we consume than what we produce. So we locate
other people, we position people in terms of their taste or
whatever. I mean it sounds awful to talk about it – I don't
particularly like it – but I think there's been a shift around
that. And, you know, consumerism's alive and well. It's one
of the more depressing things around postmodern culture:
that it hasn't really shifted, even in spite of challenges of the
environment.

Winnie: I don't know that we're not defined by the old categories of work and faith and family. There are innovations, like
a family might be queer, but the descriptions are still the same.
People are getting married. In religion people appear to have
the space to move around denominations, but I'm not seeing
much more than that.

In what sense might postmodernity impact upon the church?

Stephen: I don't think we live in as much of a free-market
society as I would like; we live in the nanny state. Anyone who
has a new idea in church, politics, society – but not in business
usually – the first thing you hear is 'Who's it going to hurt?',
not 'Who's it going to help?'

Whether there is an influence of postmodernity or not, I don't
think that is as important as the quality of our leaders. I just
don't think that we have really good leaders in the church. [That
said,] I do believe Katharine Jefferts Schori is a clear leader;
she's very clear and smart.

Callid: In the USA, people are beginning to realize that their
power and control is not infinite, which is manifesting itself
in many different ways. This loss is why the emerging church

is so predominantly white male, as they begin to realize that white men do not hold the power and control.

Sue: Culturally, people are realizing that words aren't getting through and we have to use pictures, and actually, I think, as people are brought up in a visual culture, they're less distrustful of imagery.

Roy: My fears about postmodernity are [grounded] in the so-called freedoms that it generates and propagates: we get fragmentation, and with fragmentation comes, not so much diversity, but tribalism. And if we haven't got the story to kind of cohere and help us live together, I fear that we'll become a more violent England in a postmodern culture.

Jonny: We've got blood on our hands – I suppose that's the challenge. Particularly as British Christians, and working for a mission organization, [we see that] the gospel's gone where the empire's gone. Often in places, missionaries have been great resisters of the empire, but actually, in some ways, they also opened up doorways for trade. So I think it's highly complicated. I think we have to have humility around our truth-claims, but, ironically in the postmodern world, stories and storytelling seem to be the way to communicate. So telling the Christian story of healing and redemption is fine; you just need to be round the table with other people and lose the arrogance of 'We're right, we've got the truth, you've got to get on board with us', [as] that sort of tone doesn't fit. I think that grates very badly. Yeah, I think the Christian story is very hopeful. One of the things that shifted for me was that, a lot of the ways I've been told, the Christian story seemed to be a theology of escape, [as if] eschatology sort of cuts a corner. So: 'Come to Christ and he'll rescue you from the world', or (in an extreme case) it's like a ticket to heaven and the earth's going to be destroyed. So I think, for me, discovering a different story that actually God's plan and mission is about healing, and the future of creation was to be renewed and healed, gave a very different way of kind of engaging with people. I think it's a very hopeful story, and I don't think it needs to be a dominating story.

Should the church try to relate to postmodernity, and if so, how?

Stephen: A church that isn't learning with its culture is dead, because the church is the people. In the twenty-first century, I don't really want to be part of a church that discriminates against anyone. Leadership is key: it's hopeful and forward-looking. You can trust someone to be a good leader, in the same way that a child trusts a parent who is a good parent. We want to like our leader, and we want our leaders to be good. But healthy families, congregations, communities, want their leaders to be as good as anybody else. The quality of a leader can improve the function of any kind of place.

Roy: We are more concerned as a community about communicating our values than living out any vision. We have a rule of life, a new monastic rule of life: 'availability and vulnerability'. I think they're gospel values, and my concern as an overseer of the community is to encourage people to live out the values in whichever sphere of influence God has called them. So, one of our companions is doing her doctorate; she's in the [National] Health Service and she's looking at [what] availability and vulnerability – our vows and rule of community – would look like in a GP practice. [So] that relationships matter more than reputation, medicine is about an embracing of risky living, and the litigation and fear culture that so dominates contemporary society needs to be challenged because it's getting in the way of risks.

We're just ordinary people trying to find a way for living as God's people in an exiled context, asking how to sing the Lord's song in a strange land. [We] live out a rule of life, [because] for us the gospel is quite a radical alternative life, and I think we engage with local culture by living quite alternatively and radically.

Jonny: I think, in terms of lifestyle, perhaps the most significant thing about alternative worship is its posture towards culture. You know, I think there's an undergirding, almost Catholic, theology that's sacramental, that sees God present in all of life and culture, and is discerning God within all of life and culture. And if you inhabit popular culture then there'll be whispers of that in film and music, or whatever. And that tends to be the building blocks towards worship because we don't tend to see people living a split life between 'planet church' and the rest of life. So I don't know if that's a lifestyle issue, but if you're part of the Grace community, the chances are you will think that the culture you live in, and your friends live in, is to be celebrated and affirmed; it's also to be thought about and reflected on, in terms of consumerism or whatever it is. But that tends to be the posture towards culture, which I think is great in terms of mission.

Winnie: At the beginning of the twentieth century, this neighbourhood was the heart of the anarchist movement, the socialist movement, the communist movement in the world. The rector at the time was convinced that people at the time would engage with spirituality through the arts, and he brought art into the space in the liturgy; he had dancers (which was seen as scandalous), sculpture and other art in the space. It worked in a way that was probably quite radical at the time. He tried to create liturgy around the people of this space. It was not well received, and the church reduced down to nineteen angry ladies in the congregation.

A later rector, in the 1950s, was horrified to find a black service and a white service, and he combined them; and I think everyone was mad [i.e. offended]. And he built from there. He made this place on the front lines of the civil rights movement in this neighbourhood. He invited theatre into the church, and continued the tradition of having dance in the church, which continues from the early twentieth century to this day. He continued the idea that modern people engage their spirituality through the arts, and this neighbourhood has been a hub of genre-defining arts for the twentieth century.

The church went through this struggle: is there a way to do Christian and church that is relevant? The reason places like this declined was because they did things that were radical.

How to create more intentional, multicultural spaces is something we're learning together. You're not going to come to this church if you want to default to who you know how to be most easily. At St Mark's we have a lot of people who are on the margin of something, so everyone's a little bit of an outsider. So in our community, how do we become more intentional to welcome people? We're an important voice to have at the table.

Roy: Our mission is to listen: to listen to people and to listen to culture, and hopefully to listen to God, and just listen to what's happening. We befriend people. We're not interested really in whether they join us or not, and once you get that out of the way, you can actually make genuine friendships, which is great. It's not a recruiting agency; it's actually about celebrating the dignity of human life.

Sue: I suppose it's the same as engaging with any other culture: to offer a sense of rootedness in a rootless world. And the comfort of a sense of eternal truth, while resisting that sort of cultural baggage and abuse of power that puts many people off. So it's sort of getting beyond the institution, and the walls of the institution, and the concept of power figures and control, and all those things that people are very suspicious of these days, and into transcendence and experience. Certainly with Transcendence: The Service that's what they get. That's why we've been going for very ancient chants and concepts of liturgy, and movement and ritual and candles and ancient buildings; a lot of things that other people have chucked out we're bringing back because it brings that sense of rooted-ness, while giving people choice. For example, with prayer activities, they can wander round the building and interact with what they want to interact with. We're not telling them, 'You must do this' or 'You must pray this way at this point'; there's freedom as well within that. But yeah, the thing that seems to be striking people is the rootedness, which is quite interesting.

Transcendence is a monthly multimedia mass in York Minster, and we've deliberately billed it as a mass, because we want to go for the Anglo-Catholic feel. It's got all of the high technology and DJ-ing and visuals, but it's also got creative prayer in it. There's quite often an element of movement and pilgrimage as part of the service, of going to some part of the building and interacting with prayer activities in some way, and actually using the space and the building by night. [We're] drawing upon the strengths of the Anglo-Catholic tradition; so there will be robes, there will be incense, there'll be candles, procession, movement, a sense of mystery, a sense of awe as part of it. And also, drawing on the minster's strengths along with our strengths, and mixing it up together. One of the minster's great strengths, and its biggest, is actually the building, and what a stunning resource that is! Because so many people say that the minster itself is a sacred place to them, even people that were atheist said [that] it has this affect on people when they come in. It seems to attract spiritual seekers like a magnet, which is really interesting.

The other strength: it has the liturgical strengths. We have the precentor working with us on the liturgy, so there's somebody who actually helped write *Common Worship* helping us to plan what we're doing, and because of his depth of knowledge, you know how to work stuff to its advantage and to play with it. It's clay: you can mould it, and use it to its best. And also the choristers: some of the songmen come and sing; and so you have this really interesting formulation sometimes: one minute you might have a DJ with music, and next minute someone might be singing a psalm. And there's this moment in a plainchant, where people go, 'Is that live, or is it pre-recorded?' And there's this moment where you realize that this perfectly gorgeous voice that's floating over the acoustics is actually standing in the corner, singing it on the fly.

It's been quite incredible, the range of people that it's attracted, and the range of backgrounds – and ages as well. It's the sort of thing that, on the face of it, [would make] a lot of youth workers say, 'No way would that attract teenagers!' And yet some people have brought their youth groups because they love it. And yet, at the other end of the scale, there can be retired people who are also deeply affected, and it seems to be touching people at different levels and from totally different church backgrounds. It amazes me that there's this one person who's ex-Brethren who's totally blown away by it, and also Anglo-Catholics are really happy too, and the charismatics and evangelicals, who are normally into more informal stuff, and also the random tourists, who've seen a flier or someone plugging in the lights and have decided to come along. It's really interesting. And I suspect it's something to do with this power of something that is ancient and yet renewed, because it's approachable. And I think some people really relate to the ancient and some to the renewed.

As soon as you visit, you can be part of the community, part of planning, part of this whole journey with us; it's not like you've got to wait until [you've been] with us six months, or until your theology is right, or until you've ticked some boxes, or whatever. I think Anglicanism itself provides safe-guards in terms of the lectionary and the liturgy, and also the community provides safeguards too. So it's very easy to open the doors and say, 'Come right in, come and help us.' So fuzzy boundaries are really important, and being able to come straight in is really important.

Jonny: If you work with teenagers, or whatever, if you press them on what their dream is, they want a world without racism, without suffering, without sexism, without inequality, with-out environmental damage. So [it's great] to be able to say, 'Actually, that's the Christian future.' They think it's the complete opposite, that Christianity and God doesn't like that stuff. So I think the Christian story chimes in well with the moment we're in, and can afford hope for people. But there is a lot of undoing for people, for many people. It depends, it's interesting; there are a lot of people who haven't got any engagement with the Christian story, so they'll almost hear it fresh. Whereas I think our generation have, [and] we have, to undo it for our peers.

Rather than celebrating a sort of Christian subculture, which is what the evangelical, charismatic [groups] tend to do (unwittingly, I think) [Grace's approach] was to use the stuff of everyday life and culture as the building blocks for worship, and I love that instinct, by the way. That does two things: it helps people feel like there isn't a split between their everyday life and the church; it breaks that split. But it also helps people to relocate God back in their everyday life. So you hear a track you're playing in worship, and then you're in a club and the same track's playing; you know, it kind of makes those sorts of connections.

Does that mean some models of the church should be abandoned?

Roy: Now, I think that where we, as the church and Christians, have come unstuck is we've not been able to translate that life-giving Judeo-Christian tradition in a way that relates to a change in culture, because we've imbued it with so much power and control. And we've also done it with a lack of humility. It's almost like: 'This is the way it is', and yet we haven't looked at our own houses and looked at where we need to address those issues, not least on justice issues. There is a Judeo-Christian tradition that, in a sense, provides the pectin that holds society together, but I think that people are removing the pectin; and it's no good [for] us as Christians [to be] shouting, 'You need to come back to the tradition!', because we haven't lived it well, and we need to reinterpret it. And for me, the genius of the gospel is that it can be passed on from generation to generation without being stuck in traditionalism. And in a sense, I think the task of the church is how to be gospel people in a post-Christendom, postmodern age. And the jury is out, because I think the jury is out as to what postmodernism means, the jury is out as to what post-Christendom looks like, and the jury is out as to what the gospel will look like in this changing context. But we're on that journey.

The notion that revival is the thing that is coming round the corner . . . just get real! You know? I now speak passionately about this because, you know, anybody who stands up and starts hammering on about revival is as bad as Jeremiah's contemporaries saying, 'Peace, peace', when there was no peace [see Jer. 6.14]. Soothing the people, you know? The first task of leadership, says Max De Pree, is to define reality. The reality is, the church in the West is not in revival; it's exactly the opposite. And that's where Christendom has to change, because with revivalism comes [the attitude]: 'If we just shout harder, or work harder, or just call people back to the old ways, somehow revival will come', and I just think: Why? Why, if God is true to his nature, would revival come to the West? Issues of injustice, issues where we have been blind to the realities of poverty and need, you know, gospel mandates and kingdom values – we've just violated them. And you know, for me, the whole economic recession and the crisis that the West is beginning to taste smacks much more of the judgement of God rather than [being] the forerunner of revival. I could speak for hours about that; we're not going to be able to engage with postmodernity simply by calling people back to a revival of modernity's Christendom values.

It's interesting: within monastic movements throughout the church, it seems that God has allowed a monastic movement to rise up, to call the church back to something that had been lost; calling people back to the gospel, really. I'm interested in this as a personal reflection, because when I was doing the [Baptist Union] presidency, it coincided with the Make Poverty History campaign, which fired up again my commitment to issues of social justice. But I just got really frustrated and irritated, and annoyed with myself and the church that, exposed to the reality of the facts of poverty and injustice and exploitation and slavery, as much today as in the days of Pharaoh, the church was fannying around singing songs. And I know that's a caricature, but [I want] to get people to engage with what, for me, is a gospel issue, a kingdom issue, a nature-of-God issue. I think, 'How dare we ask God to bless us in what we're doing, when we turn a blind eye to the poor, to the naked, to the neighbour in our midst, to the suffering and exploited?'

Jonny: I think Grace is interesting in terms of the journey that we've been on. If you like, the starting point for Grace might be a negative one, in that it was a struggle with the culture of church. So there were a lot of people who were either in danger of leaving church or were doing youth work to avoid church. You know, church culture, particularly the modernizing, chorus-singing [type] (whatever that was supposed to be – radical at the time), just dried up for people. It kind of became banal; it just didn't have any depth to it, particularly, you know, [if] you've got a friend who's dying of cancer, and you go to church and sing a bunch of choruses; it just didn't seem to afford depth. And the Anglican liturgy, which has got more depth to it, was also dry for different reasons, I think. So Grace was inspired by the likes of the Late, Late Service at Glasgow, which we'd encounter at [events] like Greenbelt. So they basically got permission [from the parish church] to do something new, and I think the story they told in the service was: 'If we can create worship in a way that we relate to, then we'll be able to invite our friends to it, and it won't be embarrassing or naff.' And that was the journey. Theoretically we had created something that, culturally, was much closer [to our everyday experience], and some friends would come; people joined. But actually, coming through church doors and encountering alternative worship is just as weird as singing choruses; it's just a different kind of weird. So I think that was a bit of a wake-up call for us, to think, 'Well, although we've got theoretically an incarnational theology, actually we're running Grace along attractional lines; we're still expecting [people] to come to us.' So what shifted was that we've kind of structured Grace around what we call an ethos, which is like a set of values: creativity, participation, risk and engagement. And by 'engagement' we mean engagement with the local community, or the local culture. So we scrapped meeting every week to plan worship, [because] it was almost [a realization]: 'Why would anyone want to join Grace if they didn't want to plan creative worship?' That was sort of our edge and what we did, [but] maybe there's more to life than what we did.

Callid: Many in the emerging church have been hurt in some way and are running from institutional formulations of church polity that have been damaging. I'm not trying to deny that, but at the same time I see people throwing the baby out with the bathwater. There is a lack of discipline, and in many situations the emerging church is not [an example of] neo-liberalism, but neo-individualism with a veneer of church on it. I am often saying, 'Where are your checks, communities? And what do you believe and confess?'

In the emerging church people can be so individualistic that they refuse to confess, to profess, to proclaim, and I don't believe there's any power or longitude in that church; it is very ironic: 'You can't pin me down.' I understand a lot of that movement to be a direct maladaptive to pain, injury and suffering, to a very conservative, evangelical, fundamentalist church.

So I enter in, without those experiences, saying, 'Yes, you are in pain, and distance is healing.' When night comes at the end of the long day, I do not want people to settle in that. Beyond the pain is the gospel, not the one that hurt you, but the gospel.

If people are uncomfortable professing and confessing the way they currently do those things, then, rather than not doing it, they can change the way they do it. How can you believe as opposed to not believe? At some point you have to address the Christ event and ecclesiology. Your soteriology and epistemology can be up in the air, but what is the deal with Jesus, and what are we supposed to be doing together in that memory? If we can't talk about that, then we're not an emerging church at all; we're just chit-chat.

Being 'Episco-mergent' is really not 'emergent' at all; it's simply the conversation that Episcopalians need to have with the whole denomination. It's not about having a separate emergent group, but [being] a part of the whole denomination. Making the emerging church it's own thing is not right; I don't think ecclesially that's what's occurred.

Sue: I think everyone goes through their rabid teenage phases, and I think we were probably more rabid, not about Anglicanism as such, but about very authoritarian, charismatic evangelicalism, which some of us have come out of, or had bad experiences of. So I think it was more about that which maybe sent us to explore other avenues of Anglicanism. But then again, also, there's that teenage thing that you respect your parents and learn from your parents, but you also kick against your parents in your teenage years, like: 'I don't wanna do it that way because I'm different.' I think, actually, everybody's moved. We've all grown up a bit; we don't feel like we need to be rabid teenagers any more. I'd say what's happened overall is that the Church of England has shifted, but also charismatic evangelicalism has shifted and actually brought on board [the] eating and drinking together, building community, being passionate about justice, lifestyle issues. All that sort of stuff has gone into mainstream charismatic evangelicalism, and it's moved too. Oh, and multisensory stuff too. So I think we've both moved.

People in York Minster regard Transcendence as being a fresh expression of the minster: the dean comes and celebrates [mass] and preaches sometimes, and is very involved and helpful. Up until the precentor moved in July, he was helping and planning, and the canon chancellor is now trying to take on that role. The music people too: some of the choir are coming in too. It's nice how much it is on the agenda and is a minster service rather than just us; it's more like the home team. There's a sense in which a baton is being passed from community to community; [people] want to pick up that baton and are picking up what's been good from monasticism and good from communities in the past, and in our more recent history.

Are institutional churches too heavily structured for postmodernity? Do we really need smaller, lighter, more flexible networks?

Sue: I'm more interested in the kingdom of God than in the church as an institution, if that makes sense. The church as an institution bears the kingdom of God to a greater or lesser extent; it tries to, anyway. [My big hope is] that the kingdom would grow, that the church would revitalize the country and, you know, society itself would be transformed because people would be less selfish. They wouldn't be out for themselves, but out for worshipping God within their daily lives, and serving Christ through each other and through the world around, so that the world around would be a better place to be.

Transcendence is very formal: we wear robes, we carry crosses, we have processions, although we do let people loose around the minster, round about, [at the point] where the intercession would happen in a normal service. And people absolutely love that. And even though it's very formal, actually, it reaches people, and I think one of the things we noticed was that too much informality put people off. It didn't feel like church: it was a bit scary; they didn't quite know what the ground rules were. [A youth leader] brought a load of people who loved it. I had thought, 'My goodness, what are they going to think of this?' [but] they loved it, and they're totally un-churched people. I think it's the sense of transcendence, a sense of otherness. People don't go to church because they don't think it's spiritual enough. We were trying to create that sense of otherness, of transcendence, of going into an environment where there was a sense of awe and wonder. People had chosen the Anglican tradition because of its breadth and the fact that you can do all of this wacky stuff. But also there's a sense of rootedness; within that there's a structure, and I think that actually it's easier to be free within some form of loose structure.

Winnie: I believe in creating enough structure so that people can participate; structures that are designed so that the minority person in the room can participate. Structure is more inclusive [than no structure] because it creates space and order. My dream for the place now: could we actually restore the dignity of the site, the community of the mission of Episcopal churches in urban areas, and could we do that in a way that is diverse, and progressive, and thoughtful, modelling some of the glimpses of what we believe in, and could we do it always looking outward?

[For a long time] this church has seen any user of the space as a church member, as someone who sees the church as 'theirs'. [But now we think that] if you're not a member of the Eucharistic community [at St Mark's], if you're not part of the mission of this place to serve, and if you don't contribute or offer yourself in some way; if you believe you're a member just because you come sometimes, that's actually quite a destructive place. In every way, I'm narrowing what it means to be a member of this church, intentionally. If you don't participate in the Eucharistic community of this place, and you are not being formed with us as we are formed, then you're not a member of the church. I see this as trying to [restore] the dignity of this place.

To be an Episcopalian you need to be a communicant member in good standing: you show up a lot and you pledge. From those people the vestry is made up. This church has pushed away its responsibilities, and I am trying to gather it all back in, because it's the Eucharistic community who should care enough to run all that this church does. It is from the random gathering of the Eucharistic community that we have the resources to do all that we need to do.

St Mark's has had Open Communion since the 1970s; we would probably want to have as few barriers to participation as possible. We're clear by what we mean by Communion, believing in the Real Presence [of Christ in the consecrated bread and wine], and we invite people to participate in that as they feel able.

A non-baptized person cannot, however, be a member of St Mark's. You can't be a member of St Mark's and not be a member of the Episcopal Church, because we are an Episcopal church by definition. It was once the norm for anyone who came to an Episcopal church to be made a member. However, since the ordination of women in 1976 [the denomination] has had to be more rigorous. This has been because conservative groups have steeplejacked churches: taken them over and then voted to leave the diocese. Now you have to be a baptized Episcopalian to vote at the annual meetings, and confirmed to be on the diocesan board; the constitutional canons have become very important. Part of the role is to ensure the church remains loyal to the diocese.

The reason we don't create barriers to the [Communion] Table is to tell people in this community that you are welcome to receive, that we invite you to participate. We get so many people who are beaten down about the messages of right-wing Christianity that our window [of opportunity] is 15 to 20 minutes to tell people who we are and make that invitation. We need to be aggressive about making that invitation. People are happy to be welcomed and want to get in.

Roy: I don't think Fresh Expressions has got it all. I don't think emerging church has got it all. In fact I am very concerned about aspects of the emerging church. I totally understand the reaction of the emerging church to the established church, but there are aspects of the established church that carry issues of spiritual formation that some [aspects] of the emerging church just don't have; and I think they'll burn out. You can't found something on just an idea; you've got to ask, 'What's the spirituality that's informing us?' And I think there are aspects of established church where there are some good things happening. I find it absolutely intriguing that the attendance at minsters, abbeys and cathedrals is on the rise, when most other sections of the church are waning. And I think it's about that postmodern quest for sacred space. You know, Berger, the sociologist, talks about the loss of the sacred canopy, and yet people search for the transcendent; that people find their way to places they associate with sacred canopies, [like] cathedrals, somehow seems to be the thing.

Stephen: Times Square has changed in the past 20 years from being one of the most dangerous parts of the city. The relationship between Times Square and the church has changed because there are fewer clergy working at St Mary's. I used to go to Times Square business meetings, but a lack of staff means I can't do that. St Mary's is the long-term player in Times Square: it existed before Times Square existed, and it will go on after the shops.

If that is the case, then what does the institutional church have to offer?

Winnie: Buildings in the city are not a mistake: they are a sign of where our mission should be. We cannot abandon the city, because we have these buildings; they are a gift. The money is there, the people are there, the energy is there. The problem is: can we believe in ourselves enough to actually be the kind of community God calls us to be as church? It involves a level of discipline, and discernment and help that can be counter-intuitive when you're trying to live out the passion and drive that God gives you to be who you are. Building up the least among us so that you can have space for people who don't have space, to be with the broken: this church does all of those things very well [with] the marginal of the marginal.

[Collectively] we have more voice. There is this space in the public conversation, and we can't have it individually – we have it as an institution. As church we can organize a voice that is consistent and can only grow; we can have so much more impact. The fact is, when people disengage from the institutions their parents were in, they are not disengaging from the bank, from the company that's going to pay them a big salary; their voice is heard through those institutions in the public square. What they're disengaging from is the one resource they have for social transformation. This place can speak with moral authority. The public square is a place of institutions, and we are able to challenge all of the other institutions. The gospel calls us to justice every Sunday; it's what it means to live responsibly and be connected to God. I don't see people disengaging from all institutions; they're disengaging from the ones that can make transformation. We can shout from the pulpit here. And we can model something here that is diverse, that you just don't see in the world out there.

What we are doing is working out where God is, and what God is calling us to do. How can you do that without a gathering of people? I believe in the church. At our best we are supposed to be the moral voice for society, and I think we can do that on behalf of other religions. If we don't understand that to be our task, then why do we exist? There are other voices of moral authority, but religious institutions are a part of structures, unlike casual spirituality movements. I really believe in secular governance, and true democracy is secular. But there should be a thriving and public religious life in secular society. The USA is not successful in this; minority religions do not really have any public voice. Institutions are not good in and of themselves; I think this institution could have a voice in our society, and that's why a church like this should be at the table.

Sue: Originally, I grew up in [the Roman Catholic Church] and then stomped off and kind of stripped it all down, got rid of an awful lot of it and went very ultra-evangelical, and then quite alternative, in that I stripped out that stuff as well. I mean, I'm still very biblical, but in recent years I've been moving more towards the ancient stuff, because I've realized that it is more missional than people think it is. I think we've probably chucked out the baby with the bathwater. I think it does actually speak to people. I think sometimes we can make church a café, but at the end of the day other people do cafés better than we do. So what is it *we* do? We can be a poor relation of Starbucks, or we can actually share what we really have, which is Christ.

I mean, in the Visions journey we chucked out liturgical prayers altogether, and just had songs and a talk, and actually, people coming in were expressing in some way a need to say something, but they hadn't got the words. They hadn't got the words so they needed liturgy because they needed words to say; and that was intriguing. So actually we brought it back, because we realized that throwing it out didn't work. What needed to be done was to blow the dust off it, to let it be, I suppose, reborn and renewed and relevant.

Jonny: Grace is a congregation of St Mary's Church. I mean, they have an 8 a.m., 10.30 a.m. and 6 p.m. [service], and we're another one of those in their minds, I think. And we prefer to be connected than separate. The track record of [groups] that go off and do their own thing is a little depressing. So we prefer to be linked into the wider church. Some of the people [at Grace] are on the electoral roll; some probably don't know what an electoral roll is – that doesn't cross their radar – and we don't particularly push that system much.

One thing that we focus on tends to be the rhythm of the church year. So it would be normal that we're visiting Advent and Christmas. Lent tends to be a focus for us, as well as Easter, Pentecost and sometimes Trinity; it depends slightly on the month these things fall in. So we like that rhythm of the church year.

Does any of this connect with the broader philosophical conversation about postmodernism?

Roy: I think what postmodernity has done is given me the freedom to say, 'Actually, I'm not so sure.' It's enabled me to be more true to who I am, actually more true to my heart. And of course it's more vulnerable, but that's one of our rules of life, anyway, so I'm stuck with that one. It's enabled me to be more honest. That doesn't mean I was a lying preacher, but there were just occasions when issues of conscience emerged for me, when I was doing the stuff and just feeling, 'I'm actually not sure I believe this stuff; even though there's some evidence to say this stuff works, I'm not sure I believe it.' I think postmodernity has given me freedom and permission to question assumptions, to be a little bit more unsure about things. The irony is that my love of God has deepened through that process.

Postmodernity has made me much less propositional and truth-statement-ing, and much more exploratory and story[-oriented]. [I have read] that one of our tasks in a postmodern culture is, in the midst of all the endearing myths, to tell the enduring story.' But telling the story is different from haranguing people with huge, great propositional truth statements that they've got to buy into.

Callid: First, my position is that modernism and postmodernism are contemporaneous. Postmodernism suggests, though, a movement towards [realizing that] marginalized epistemologies have something to bring. Post-Lyotard, we've gone awry by reascribing metaphysics to it. The keen insight Lyotard made is about media and epistemology.

When I'm in a conversation with a conservative Christian, I don't think there is anything they're not getting. They're not wrong or missing something; their worldview is [just] significantly different from mine.

Modernism and postmodernism have a great deal in common with one another, but there are some important things that are different. They are not at loggerheads; I don't buy it. Postmodernism is a very subtle move.

If theology is the human response to the reception of grace, and postmodernism is the movement towards accepting marginalized voices, then there can be such a thing as postmodern theology. A postmodern theology would be a theology that is a response to the new things God is giving to the children of God, and dialectically hearing the way people are responding to it: this is the traditional perspective. This is how my conversation with that tradition can be explained, and how, given that my view is different, we can work out what to do with that difference. The function of the postmodern theologian is far more about hosting a conversation that is ongoing than it is about concluding a conversation. Postmodern theology is not just about new content, but a methodological shift, because otherwise you're doing modern theology but saying edgy stuff.

Jonny: Well, I tend to use 'postmodern' as a cultural descriptor, so I like the phrase, 'postmodern times'. David Lyon uses it in his books: it's the water we're swimming in; it's the air that we breathe. That tends to be what I mean by postmodern, I suppose. I mean, for me, it's what comes after what was before: modernity. Modernity would be characterized by the myth of progress: 'Science technology, you're gonna make the world a better place – the promised land, riches for all!' etc., etc. But I think that, for a lot of us, that myth we just don't believe any more. So it's like the rug's been pulled from under our feet; that worldview collapsed for a lot of people, or the certainties of that have collapsed. So postmodernity is what comes after that, and I think it's characterized by suspicion of too much certainty and truth-claims in that sort of way. I mean, things that characterize it for me: some of the themes would be around truth. I like the postmodern stuff, I have to say, around truth, because truth is embedded or contextual, so I can only see or have a take on truth from where I'm standing at a particular time. I see the world from where I'm standing: objective truth isn't available to me. I haven't got the big 'modern' thing, objective facts or whatever. So, minimally, I need to have humility around my truth-claims, and I think that's been backed up by the feeling that, in terms of theology, people have made truth-claims that have come undone, I suppose. They've been too arrogant and dominant. So truth turns out to be much more complex than the way I think things are from my perspective. I like that – it sort of calls for a humility around our truth-claims – but we're much more likely to get at the truth if we sit around the table with a range of voices. I mean that closely relates to the idea – the 'Ephesians moment', I think – that we only understand who Christ is as we see the many faces of Christ around the world. So I think that will be one of the strong themes in postmodernity: suspicion of truth-claims, but a very different way of, then, wanting to unpack truth. I don't think it means the truth doesn't exist.

[End of conversations]

* * *

In sharing excerpts of my interviews with these six church leaders, I hope to have demonstrated that using 'emergent' as a way of defining churches and people is not as helpful a description as some have previously suggested. Not only are there enormous overlaps between the different church leaders, but also those within emerging groups cannot simply be said to be assimilating Catholic practices into low church Protestantism. For example, in adding informality and modern music to services and increasing congregational participation, Sue has as much to do with modern Catholic liturgical renewal as anything necessarily 'emerging'.

As well as a lack of clarity, there are also some important differences that are worth noting. First, Roy's and Stephen's responses to free-market capitalism, for example, are notably different. Second, the way in which Christianity might be understood as a big project with a big story is handled quite differently by the different church leaders. A third difference is in the way the leaders present the story of their churches. Both Sue and Jonny explain that it was dissatisfaction with a local church that motivated them to form their church groups. While Callid agrees that this is often the case in emerging churches, he is concerned that there is also a great deal of hurt that has motivated these moves. Callid believes, like Donald Carson, that talking about God and the church may have become a way to hide from dealing with this hurt.

While I had expected to find such complexity and difference in such a wide group of church leaders, there were also some surprises. For example, the relationships these church leaders have with various denominational institutions is far more favourable than I had expected. While it may not be overly surprising to hear an Episcopalian speak favourably of the church as an institution (as Winnie does), I had not expected her to be so emphatic about the importance of the institution. Further, it was surprising to hear Roy, from a nonconformist background, speak so warmly about the established church in England. Equally, while I was not surprised to hear of the importance ascribed to welcoming all people, I had not expected this to be coupled with a sense of 'guarding' the ethos of the church groups. Roy, Jonny and Winnie particularly expressed their understanding that, for a group to be open to all, such an ethos needs protecting if it is to be sustained.

Such complexities, differences and surprises lead me to conclude that if a person is searching for the emerging church as a single, identifiable entity, then they will be disappointed: this emerging church does not exist. I am not convinced that there is enough evidence in any research project to suggest a clear difference between the so-called inherited and emerging churches. There are too many similarities between these two descriptions of the church, both in their practices and beliefs. Of course there are differences between Roy Searle's Northumbria Community and Stephen Gerth's St Mary's Church, Times Square; but are these differences best characterized as emerging–inherited, or in terms of the much older difference between low church Protestantism and high church Anglicanism? There are certainly developments within those denominations, and they may well be embodied by Roy Searle and Stephen Gerth, but that does not provide the evidence to substantiate the kind of emerging–inherited narrative proffered by many narrators of the emerging church. Perhaps the strongest evidence for such a narrative can be seen in the way these two groupings are said to understand and expect participation in the life of the church.

Emerging churches are said to have a greater degree of inclusivity and participation because of the way anyone, whether a 'member' or not, is able to be active within the worship and social life of the church. Common threads to the kinds of narratives shared by those within these groups are regular worship-planning meetings (which are open to all), an interactive approach to 'sermons' that attempt to move away from the style of a monologue, the practice of Open Communion, and interactive, often tactile, methods of intercession. To what extent, however, do these practices actually demonstrate a greater degree of inclusivity and participation than other forms of the church? The high level of informality, tactile styles of interaction, and high levels of technology mean that the movement is inclusive only to those for whom such things are appealing. Indeed, this is something that has been realized by both Jonny Baker ('encountering alternative worship is just as weird as singing choruses; it's just a different kind of weird') and Sue Wallace ('too much informality put people off'). More than that, however, suggesting that this approach is more participative than the 'inherited' church is rather misleading, as the functioning of any church requires an enormous amount of participation. It is surely more accurate not to say that 'emerging' groups are more participative, but that they operate under a different model of participation. Winnie Varghese's comment proves salient at this point: that participation is not necessarily a good in and of itself, as completely open participation would leave a church vulnerable to losing its distinctive ethos were people with opposing views to join.

This is not to say that there are not observable differences in the church in the postmodern condition, but that I find the new–old, inherited–emerging narrative problematic, having its origin most likely in the politics of a particular church rather than in an attempt to understand what is actually going on. It is this 'branding' that I find so distasteful in the work of various narrators of the emerging church, as it seems to serve to segregate churches unfairly according to a rather superficial analysis, when they actually share a great deal in common. Within these narratives, the branding of a particular group as either inherited or emerging serves either to patronize or demonize it in the effort then to promote a particular point of view, whether that be, for example, radical orthodoxy or 'pyro-theology'. Far from resourcing the church in the postmodern condition, this has distracted the church and engaged it in debates, practices and structural reorganizations based upon a narrative that is only superficially related to reality, if at all.

Some narrators prefer to speak of the emerging church as a conversation rather than as an organization, which suggests that what I am saying should not come as a surprise. The writers of the previous chapter, and the church leaders in this chapter, reveal to me that 'the emerging church' is best understood as a dialogue that has been created (accidentally or otherwise) by groups who have expressed particular views concerning the relationship between the church and the postmodern condition. The tension between the various views has drawn in people and groups who are exploring these issues in discussion and practice, giving rise to an energetic and creative conversation. In the next two chapters I will explain this in more depth in order to outline the dynamics of the church in the postmodern condition, as well as to suggest some ways forward.

4

Mapping the church in the postmodern condition

———————•◦•———————

Having listened to the leaders of various churches in the UK and USA, as well as reading works that discuss the church and the postmodern condition, I am led to believe that mapping these groups is less difficult than I first thought it might be. There are three topics of debate in the dialogues about the church and the postmodern condition: the church and postmodernism; the church and postmodernity; the church as institution. These three topics have generated some strong feelings, and there is a tension between the polar opinions that has become filled with lively debates and practical explorations of each set of ideas. Should the church be learning from the wisdom of postmodern philosophy, or is such an idea abhorrent and impossible for the church formed on the revelation of Jesus Christ? Should the church stand in judgement of the superficiality of postmodern cultures, or can the church learn from the insights of postmodernity? As an institution, is the church part of the solution, or part of the problem? These questions provide the very energy of what has become known as the emerging church movement.

Before moving on to the specifics, one more thing needs to be made clear: these tensions are not 'new'. As I said in the opening chapter, they are tensions with which the church has lived since its origin; they have always been present, and they will never go away. The relationship of the church to culture and society, to philosophy, to other institutions, as well as the way in which the church understands itself as an institution are issues present in the writings of St Paul onwards. What I am intending to do is to discuss these tensions as they exist in the postmodern context, describing the works of those who stand at either end of the debates, and how these tensions can be seen in the practices of the churches.

The church and postmodernism

How does theology develop: by discussing only its own historical writings and Scriptures, or by engaging with ideas from outside its own traditions? Two thinkers who represent either end of this tension are Donald Carson and Peter Rollins. While this may appear to be a philosophical discussion that belongs solely in university seminar rooms, it is actually a critical debate. For instance, if the Scriptures contain everything that is needed for living faithfully as a Christian in the present world, then what about those contemporary issues that the biblical writers could never have imagined? Moving beyond the Scriptures to embrace the whole of orthodox Christian teaching, is it possible to observe that the Christian tradition has a specific and unique way of thinking that is different from everyone else's? In becoming a disciple, must one reject 'the world's' ways of thinking, and be nurtured in a distinctive Christian philosophy? In contrast to this, however, one could argue that the Scriptures and church teachings are actually as contextual and limited as all other forms of human thinking, so relating to wider philosophical thought is vital for the integrity and relevance of the church. Carson and Rollins help bring this tension into relief.

Donald Carson

For Donald Carson, whose view of Christianity is tied up with submission to absolute truth, postmodern philosophy presents a particular challenge. His concern is that Christians are being lured away from right thinking by atheistic patterns of thought; he wishes to critique this tendency and call them back to the truth. The main concern that Carson has about postmodernism is twofold: that its method is atheistic, and that as a philosophy it is inconsistent. He argues, first, that it is atheistic because its 'starting point' is not with God, but with 'I'. This, he says, is true of both modern and postmodern philosophies, and Christianity stands against this egocentric approach as 'an omniscient, talking God changes everything'.[1] On this point, Carson attempts to align himself with what he calls 'pre-modern' thought, in which the only knowledge that existed came through revelation from God.[2] His second major criticism is that postmodern thinking is inconsistent: by insisting that there cannot be any single truth, or that there are no rights and wrongs, it undermines its own argument, which relies on being right and true. This, Carson argues, is not only absurd, but quickly becomes arrogant.[3] So different are they in approach and method that there cannot be any dialogue between this philosophy and Christianity, only conflict.

For Carson, being a Christian cannot be separated from 'adhering to the truth'.[4] This truth is the absolute truth that is contained in Scripture[5] and can be known objectively, and in this truth the Christian is to seek to make sense of his or her experiences. This truth is trustworthy not only because it is 'stabilized by constant review', established upon historical witness and grounded in biblical revelation, but because this whole process was 'super-intended' by God.[6] Carson is keen to point out that 'objective truth' has too often been rejected because it has been confused with 'omniscient truth'. He argues that one can really know things with confidence (objectively), without knowing everything, and that this is how knowledge most often works.[7]

Carson is particularly concerned that postmodernism 'glories in diversities' rather than seeking after truth,[8] because he believes that relativism is simply not an option for Christians.[9] Absolutes must exist, he argues, as Jesus himself calls for absolute submission;[10] while the way the truth is spoken or thought about will always be culture-dependent, the truth being articulated remains true.[11] Since absolute truth has such a prominent position in Christianity, the relativism that Carson sees in postmodernism can be nothing other than a threat. To even entertain a dialogue with such a philosophy would be corrosive to the church and discipleship, which is why Carson sees it as necessary to take such a strong stand against both postmodernism and any church that has sought to align itself with any of its patterns of thought.

Peter Rollins

While there are a number of groups and writers that would consider themselves to oppose Carson's work on many different fronts, Peter Rollins seems to bring this approach to life regarding Carson's views on postmodernism. Identifying himself as a philosopher, Rollins's work in his books, talks, groups and blog is an attempt to start a radical movement that embraces the insights of postmodernism and destroys the church as we know it. The detail of his interaction with postmodernism is rich, varied and sometimes entertaining, and there are three aspects to his whole approach that place him at odds with the conservative evangelical approach presented by Carson. I would name these as: (1) orthodoxy is heretical; (2) there is a need to return to the Christ event; and (3) postmodernism is Christianity's critical friend.

Rollins's view of the church throughout history is of a shifting, changing, morphing collective of people and groups who have been disturbed and inspired by the Christian presentation of God to live a life that is characterized by love. This unsettled understanding of the church leads Rollins to reject the idea of orthodoxy, as such a concept is an attempt to tether something that cannot be kept still. More than that, Rollins argues that orthodoxy is skewed in the same way as history: it is always written by the victors. Such a move has caused the church to lose its precious unsettled nature and become a place of safety. Such stability makes Christianity impossible.

Against this tendency to orthodoxy, Rollins intends to show that 'new theological configurations are possible'. While these will be 'new' because of the context of the contemporary world, Rollins insists that this approach, and not orthodoxy, has been the nature of the church throughout history.[12] Rollins is as direct and uncompromisingly committed to this as Carson is to his conservative evangelicalism. It is Rollins's vision to see the church resurrected through his project of insurrection against orthodoxy and institution (the latter of which I will discuss later in this chapter).[13]

Rollins is keen to point out that his move against orthodoxy should not be confused with a simple desire to return to the early church; he does not accept that returning to various points in history in order to recreate some ideal will have any benefit for the church in its current form. Indeed, such a move would undermine his orthodoxy-as-heresy project, suggesting as it does that there was a time when the church was right. Rollins's intention is not at all to reinvent the early church, but to return to the Christ event itself. Rollins argues that it is only through the church's continual return to this event that the church is able to realize its potential.[14]

This is all foundational to Rollins's understanding that theology is not a hermetically sealed way of thinking that is closed off from the rest of the world. Rather, theology is forever changing in response to its context, and that naturally includes the philosophical context. For Rollins, just as the philosophies that have been active in shaping the world are being challenged by postmodernism, so this is the case for theology. It is in this sense that Rollins sees postmodernism as theology's friend, albeit a critical one.

An example will help illustrate what has led me to use this phrase. Often, Rollins's work makes reference to various philosophers, and Slovenian philosopher Slavoj Žižek appears to be a particularly strong influence. On one page of his blog, having told one of Žižek's funnier jokes, Rollins suggests that belief is often used to give eternal significance and cosmic meaning to things that individuals consider to be important. The Big Other (that is, 'God') is just an invented character with whom a person can share their successes, and who can fill their life's choices with meaning. Rollins suggests that while these criticisms of belief may, at first, seem damning of Christianity, he believes that Christianity can actually be seen to resist, subvert and even undermine this challenge. While Christian orthodoxy would insist that Jesus is Lord and is seated on the heavenly throne, Rollins suggests that a more careful reading of Christianity speaks differently of God. For Rollins, an enthroned God is too otherworldly compared to the One who was made flesh; rather, it is in material acts of love in a material world that 'one affirms the God of Christianity'. It is only because Rollins has listened to, discussed with and learned from philosophers such as Žižek that he is able to affirm that there is no God who acts as the Big Other, filling an otherwise empty life with meaning. Rather, God, who is not the Big Other, is experienced in the sharing of love in this life. In this sense, postmodernism is not a threat to Christianity; rather it presents an opportunity for the church to rework its theology and its understanding of salvation.[15]

Radical orthodoxy

Placing the work of Carson and Rollins together allows me to present a particularly straightforward tension between two opposite poles. Where Carson yells at people, 'Stand back; there's nothing to see here', Rollins invites the church: 'Say hello to my critical friend.' There is, however, a third position that does not belong in the 'middle ground' between Rollins and Carson. While the radical orthodoxy movement engages with postmodernism, it does so in a very different way from Rollins. Whereas Rollins has attempted to construct dialogue that errs towards the agendas of postmodernism, radical orthodoxy attempts to engage according to its own theological agenda. This movement began out of frustration, not merely with the liberal project of the twentieth century, but with the whole modern project that began in the Middle Ages. John Milbank, one of radical orthodoxy's most outspoken protagonists, forcefully insists that a mistake was made in the thirteenth century, when Duns Scotus separated philosophy from theology. Rather than seeing theology as the discipline that gave meaning and context to all other disciplines, philosophy was said to exist according to its own logic and practices, which did not depend upon theology. Milbank argues that such a separating of philosophy from theology actually cut it off from its source (that is, cut it off from God), making philosophy atheistic.[16]

Unlike Carson, however, Milbank does not want to reject postmodern philosophy outright, but rather engage with it on his own terms. Once philosophy has been put back in its place, as a subdiscipline of theology, then radical orthodoxy is happy to engage and reconfigure postmodernism. One of the places in which the radical orthodoxy approach to postmodernism is most succinctly laid out is in a chapter by Christian Bauerschmidt in *Radical Orthodoxy*, itself a book intended to present radical orthodoxy as a coherent movement.

A key idea within radical orthodoxy is that philosophy without theology is flawed, meaningless and self-destructive,[17] which Bauerschmidt carefully explores in his article. In engaging with Jean-François Lyotard, a hugely important figure in postmodernism, Bauerschmidt attempts to demonstrate two things: why philosophy-divorced-from-theology is flawed; and, by rooting Lyotard's ideas in theology, how postmodernism can move beyond mere suspicion.[18] Bauerschmidt argues that, on its own, Lyotard's philosophy is a godless anarchy that makes everything meaningless and further divides humanity. Within a radical orthodoxy framework, however, Lyotard's ideas can be translated from atheism into Christianity, and so transformed to enable a deeper understanding of Christ and his church.[19]

The thinkers behind radical orthodoxy seek to present a clear contrast between theology, which is able to plumb the depths of existence, and atheistic philosophy, which they claim to be condemned to superficiality and confusion. While this is certainly a rejection of any way of thinking that is outside the theological, it does not lead these radical orthodoxy thinkers to the same kind of conflict as is experienced by followers of Carson's conservative evangelicalism. Rather than rejecting wholesale whatever postmodernism has to offer, they seek 'to reclaim the world by situating its concerns and activities within a theological framework'.[20] This is not dialogue in the way Rollins would recognize it, as it insists too much upon following its own rules. Nor can it really be thought of as a 'middle ground' between Rollins and Carson, as its own method is too different from both of these approaches really to be described as inhabiting such a position. It is, rather, a position that complicates the tension that I am trying to present. It sits closer to Rollins than Carson in its engagement with postmodernism, yet its view of theology forces a tension with Rollins's approach that appears to hold theology either alongside, or under, philosophy. An uneven triangle of tensions, then, is what is formed by these three approaches that seek to understand the church in relation to postmodernism: a point of conflict, a point of critical dialogue, and a point of translation.

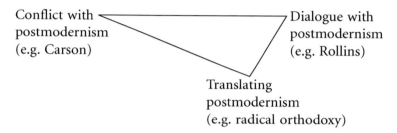

Conflict with
postmodernism
(e.g. Carson)

Dialogue with
postmodernism
(e.g. Rollins)

Translating
postmodernism
(e.g. radical orthodoxy)

The church and postmodernity

The second tension involves the church's relationship to society and culture. Is the church somehow separated from the socio-cultural changes of the wider world, or is it simply another human group that is as susceptible to these changes as any other group? Must the church change its language, habits, practices and beliefs in order to remain relevant, or should it stand on its historic principles to offer the world salvation from itself? While these issues are certainly not divorced from the way the church's relationship to postmodern philosophy is understood, there are interesting differences in the stances of certain groups and people. As I shall discuss in a moment, where radical orthodoxy will engage with postmodernism (albeit on its own terms), its writers speak out most vociferously against any dialogue with postmodernity. Equally, Rollins, who believes theology has much to learn from postmodernism, is almost as hostile to postmodernity as the radical orthodoxy movement. This section will begin, however, with a brief presentation of the work of Pete Ward, who believes that the church should embrace postmodernity.

Pete Ward

As I explained in Chapter 2, Pete Ward believes postmodernity is something to be embraced, as it presents opportunities to re-imagine ways for the church 'to be an effective agent for mission within liquid modernity'.[21] For Ward, a liquid society in which the market is given free rein is no more of a threat to the church than any other socio-cultural way of being. Through his reading of Baudrillard, Bauman and cultural commentator John Fiske, Ward states that consumerist culture has empowered individuals to construct their own lives as they see fit, rather than being controlled by institutions, businesses and the free market.[22] In this sense, consumerism is said to provide the pattern for life in the postmodern condition, and is to be welcomed as an improvement upon previous hierarchical societies.[23] Ward argues that the church should stop condemning consumerism as shallow or harmful, but rather 'as a spiritual exercise' through which individuals are attempting to explore and express themselves.[24] Equally, production and consumption are no longer merely economic terms, but are key ways of understanding how people understand their own identities in the world, buying 'things' and joining groups as part of that search.

The role of theology, then, is not to critique this practice, but to learn to live within it. More than that, it is to learn to use its language in order to free the church and its own discourses from 'solid' cultural practices in order to be engaged with society within liquid modernity.[25] The practical impact is for the church to become a network rather than a congregation, in which 'worshippers are free to shop', gravitating towards those leaders whom 'they perceive as being enlightened and in the know'.[26] While this may take the form of physical gatherings, it is more likely to be organized electronically, so that people meet more often in the virtual world than they do in any other form. Through these networks and gathering hubs, Ward challenges the church to stop meeting people's needs, and instead begin 'stimulating their desires'.[27]

Radical orthodoxy

The radical orthodoxy movement takes an entirely opposite position to Ward, often harshly criticizing the 'liquid church' approach. Despite their cautious engagement with postmodernism, the proponents of radical orthodoxy completely reject socio-cultural postmodernity. In its openness to free-market expansion and the importance placed upon consumerism and individualism, postmodernity is described as 'soulless, aggressive, nonchalant and nihilistic'.[28] Such cultures, in which time and space are understood solely in terms of productivity, can only define the worth of a human person and their communities according to their potential to increase capital. This leads to postmodern society being presented as a place of violent competition that breeds such militant individualism that it is utterly hostile to the Christian idea that humanity might participate in God and one another.[29]

Given such a negative view of postmodernity, it should be of no surprise that radical orthodoxy believes that the only Christian response is one of conflict and rejection. According to this movement, the church has a calling to judge all cultures by its own standards, and this is particularly relevant to the rampant secularism of postmodernity.[30] Any attempts at dialogue or inculturation are seen as naive, and said to lead to the secularizing, and ultimate demise, of the church. Radical orthodoxy calls the church to see postmodernism as toxic, and to recognize that it is only in the Christian community itself that Christian virtues can be developed when living amid such a godless society.[31]

However, radical orthodoxy is not simply a reaction against the contemporary postmodern condition; rather, it seeks to be a wholesale rejection of the entire modern, secular project, of which postmodernity is simply an extension and intensification. As with its stance regarding postmodern philosophy, if something is not framed theologically, then it is grounded apart from God, literally in nothing.[32] While its adherents argue this to be true of the many capital-driven corporations, it is also said to be no less true of the state, which is defined as a meaningless imitation of the church.[33] While the state may talk of justice and peace, radical orthodoxy argues that the secular state has never been able to deliver such claims when God is not worshipped.[34]

John Milbank sees a direct continuation between contemporary secular thought and that of ancient belief, wherein humanity and the world are deemed to be so chaotic that they must be tamed, like a pack of wild animals. This taming is what Milbank calls an 'original violence', the contemporary version of which is brought about through the rules of market economics and nation states.[35] To suggest, then, that Christendom should engage, and even learn from, secularism is to become a partner in this violence. Rather, Milbank believes that the only way to critique capitalism is from within an alternative big project formed by a different big story.[36]

This Christendom is said to be the natural result of God interrupting history by becoming incarnate in Christ.[37] In doing so, the church was formed as the only reconciled society, and all those who enter into Christ through baptism also enter into the peace and social order of Christendom.[38] Christendom is understood as a separate order from anything else in the world's societies as it is uniquely placed within the big story of God's engagement with the world through Christ. No other social structure, however virtuous, can belong in any way to this story: salvation is found in Christendom alone.[39] It does not exist to convert secularism, but to be the 'other city', which is formed, and lives, according to its own story.[40]

The proponents of radical orthodoxy paint a very clear choice between their own position of Christendom and the collapse of Christianity. The lack of middle ground suggests that there is, or at least should be, a sense of urgency within the church to pull out of any engagement with postmodernity, such is the intensity of its militant secularism. The contrast with the work of Pete Ward, then, could not be more striking. Within his view, postmodernity is viewed as just another day in the development of the world. There is no reason to fear postmodernism, any more than there was to fear any other point in time. What is to be feared, according to Ward, is that the church will refuse to change along with the world. Such a positioning will leave the church out of touch not only with its context, but also with God who is active in the world. The church does not exist to defend or judge any cultural context, as they are all neutral; rather, the role of the church is to be present in every social situation throughout the world. In the midst of this tension, one is left wondering whether seeking to be relevant is a search to be faithful, or whether relevance is nothing more than chasing after the false and hubristic gods of one's age.

The church as institution

The final tension that I believe gives energy to the kinds of movements and discussions associated with the church and the postmodern condition is how the church itself is understood as an institution. As I said at the beginning of this discussion, none of these tensions are new, but are contemporary versions of debates as old as the church itself. While it is fairly unremarkable to say that the church is an institution, the tension that I wish to outline arises out of two polar visions of what to do with that statement. While radical orthodoxy and the position outlined by Peter Rollins can be said to be fairly similar regarding postmodernism and postmodernity, they are poles apart when it comes to their thinking about the church as institution. Whereas radical orthodoxy would like to strengthen the church's institutionalism, Peter Rollins would like to destroy it. These polar positions have, quite wrongly, become known as inherited–emerging, as a way of naming the difference between the two approaches. This terminology is inappropriate because it is simply inconceivable to speak of the church that is somehow not inherited; the very nature of the church, the gospel, the doctrines and creeds are things that are handed on. Further, the use of the word 'inherited' as a derogatory synonym for 'maintaining the status quo' does a great disservice to the radical orthodoxy project, which is certainly hoping to see a great change in the church. The use of 'inherited' in this way also misrepresents the position occupied by Peter Rollins as being entirely new; while Rollins uses interesting terms such as pyro-theology and heretical orthodoxy, in relation to the church-as-institution his approach shares a great deal of similarity with historic nonconformism. While many supposedly nonconformist churches in the USA and UK have become more focused upon issues of personal faith and lifestyle, Peter Rollins[41] would appear to be more recognizable as an inheritor of the historic nonconformist vision. That is not to say, however, that neither Rollins nor radical orthodoxy have anything new to say on the matter; the tension may well be recognizable as the choice between Christendom and nonconformism, but the ideas and language are grounded within the contemporary context.

Peter Rollins

Rollins believes that such are the abuses in the church that one should desire to see it implode. The origin of these abuses lies neither with Christ, nor the Christ event, but entirely with the church, which has been neither radical nor faithful enough truly to enter into the space opened up by the Christ event. At some point there was a failure to act, which has resulted in the rotting of the church.[42] This rotten church is understood by Rollins to give us two options: God is either a product that gives people's lives meaning; or if one can't quite believe that, then the church's structure and liturgy will say that for them, acting as a comfort blanket to keep them safe from themselves and the world. Rollins believes that these options can be observed in various ways within the contemporary church.

First, he argues that the function of a priest is to act and believe on behalf of the church, to do, or simulate, what the people need to see and hear in order to feel safe. As well as priests, church architecture itself is said to be complicit in speaking on behalf of people. Both of these examples are an attempt to show how the practices, structures, people and the very institution and being of the contemporary church hinder honesty, and dull radicalism.[43]

If the church is rotten because of a failure to act, then, insists Rollins, the solution is to 'repeat' the church. That is to say that by identifying the moment of failure, and acting where the church previously failed to act, we will enable the church to be the church once more. Rollins admits that this is a highly risky idea, knowing that if such an action does not succeed, then the church will once again be based on failure and be as rotten as 'the institution we attempt to overthrow'. So great are the failures of the contemporary church, however, that Rollins believes that such a move is worth the risk so that people might enter more fully into the Christ event.[44]

In many ways, Rollins's 'pyro-theology' can be seen to work like a Grand Inquisitor that questions and interrogates the church, asking it to be brave enough to see itself as it is, so that it might be purged of its offences and enter again into the Christ event. This event, which is so central to Rollins's understanding of the potentiality of the church, is to encounter the crucifixion in such a way that it is allowed to be transformative, stripping away the desire for security and confronting people with themselves and one another. Neither priest, liturgy nor building can do this on someone's behalf; the individual must take responsibility for his or her own transformation. Through such an encounter, it is Rollins's hope that the church will be ruptured, reconfigured and overturned in all of its current forms, so that it might become utterly different and yet true to its previous incarnations.

Key to this church are leaders who refuse to lead and priests who refuse priesthood. Rather than enacting anything on the behalf of others, responsibility is 'pushed' on to the whole congregation. The priest is the one who refuses to give people the kind of security and safety they desire, insisting that people participate themselves.[45] For Rollins, without this form of anti-leadership the church will only ever continue to repeat the mistakes of the past, and thus fail to enable people to enter into the radical nature of the Christ event. The other side to this is that, as Katharine Moody has eloquently stated, not only does the church need 'the leader who refuses to lead' but also 'the people who refuse to be led'.[46] This appears to encapsulate an important part of Rollins's project: to move beyond the false categories of priest–lay and leader–led, in order to see the whole company of the faithful entering into the space that has been created by the Christ event. The only way in which this will take place, according to Rollins, is through his pyro-theology, which will burn the current, rotten church institution to the ground.

Radical orthodoxy

Put as crudely as possible, radical orthodoxy maintains that the institution of the church is the church, and the church can be no other. It is the unique, self-sufficient (in relation to the state) geographical and communal institution in which God's love can be known and shared. To follow Rollins's pyro-theology would be seen as naive, at best, and more likely as an heretical, pointless and dangerous move that would threaten the church and inadvertently collude with the state.

According to John Milbank, the church is found only in its sacred, consecrated buildings, which 'image' the whole cosmos and history in a way that no other place is able to.[47] While church people may frequent coffee shops, skateboarding parks and knitting clubs, the church cannot be found in those places as they cannot hold the fullness of God incarnate. It is only in the church's buildings that people can come together as human persons, without political, economic or religious labels.[48] Far from being a security blanket, the church's buildings are the only places on earth where a person is able to be connected to the true and full humanity that was revealed through the Incarnation.[49]

Each of these church buildings belongs to a church parish, which is the church's way of mapping the world. For Milbank, there can be no other way for the church to understand its world without falling into private, voluntarist, exclusive clubs; the parish is entirely inclusive because everyone who lives in that place is in the church's care. Further, it is this inclusive geography of the church, and not the separatist nationalism of states, that will become the same space as the redeemed cosmos.[50] As Davison and Milbank have pointed out, far from being a burden to mission, the buildings of the church are an inseparable part not only of the church's mission, but also of its identity.[51]

The buildings and parishes are local manifestations of the universal church, which is, according to radical orthodoxy, a spiritual society that existed before, and continues to exist apart from, the secular states. For the church to collude with the nation states or the free market is to force Christianity to deny itself. Rather, Christianity is to be understood as Christendom, and to understand it as anything less is said to make a lie of the Incarnation.[52] Through the dying to self enacted in baptism, one enters the city of peace in which all divisions, such as nation and gender, are genuinely obliterated under a democracy guarded by a holy hierarchy of bishops, priests and deacons.[53] The church as institution is the institution of God's reconciliation, and the two are inseparable; to give up on the church as institution is to give up on the church itself, and to allow the state and the market victory over the church.[54]

Conclusion

In attempting to understand the church and the postmodern condition, writers have created three sets of tensions: the church's relationship with postmodernism, with postmodernity, and with itself as an institution. While the polarized views have certainly caused some parts of the church to divide, this has not been the norm. Instead, these tensions have energized practices and stimulated thinking to stir the church into considering its identity and its relation to the world.

Chapter 3 demonstrates that the church leaders with whom I have met occupy much more complex positions than those writers I have just outlined; I certainly would not place any of them at the poles of any of the tensions. It would be easy to suggest that the complexity of the debates has led church leaders to either confusion or apathy, which is why they prefer to occupy the middle ground. This, though, would be an unfair interpretation of these leaders. The rich language they use demonstrates a depth to their understanding of these matters, suggesting that there is a great deal of thought behind the positions they have taken.

Within the writings of these leaders, there is a greater use of nuance in order to understand themselves and the world than there appears to be at either ends of the three tensions. The way they exist within these tensions demonstrates that the leaders present a greater complexity in the way they understand people and groups to be constituted, with dialogue and contradiction being more commonplace than the more polarized thinkers would appear to be able to accept. That is not to say that the narrators with whom I have engaged are 'wrong' in any way, but that there is a different view being presented by the church leaders with whom I have met. It is important to ask, however, whether this supposedly more 'nuanced' thinking (a pejorative term if ever I used one) is actually more negative than I am suggesting: whether, rather than using nuance, these are spineless leaders who simply can't make up their minds.

I use the word 'spineless' deliberately, as it is the central criticism of postmodernity made by Zygmunt Bauman in his book, *The Art of Life*.[55] Bauman believes that the one constant in postmodernity is that all people and groups insist on their right to be flexible, free to choose who they want to be, even if such identities are contradictory. Further, if an old identity has become difficult to bear, then it can be cast off for something new. This, says Bauman, is a 'spineless' way of constructing identity that lacks any sense of character.[56] As a criticism it speaks directly to the superficial floating through the world that is particularly prevalent in those who seek their own success.

I am not convinced, however, that this would be a good summary of the leaders with whom I have met. What was presented was never laissez-faire regarding their opinions, as if they would change depending upon the audience they were addressing. There was no suggestion, as far as I could see, that these leaders simply believed they needed to be 'relevant', in the sense that being popular is more important than being faithful. Rather, the faith was presented as something that existed in dialogue, not only with its own history, but also with the world beyond the church. Whether it was about gender roles or having humility around truth-claims, lessons from free-market economics or institutionalism, the language and practice of the faith had been enriched, not impoverished, by the postmodern condition in which these leaders lived.

Such an understanding of the faith rejects separatism, unlike the anti-postmodernity of radical orthodoxy, the anti-postmodernism of conservative evangelicalism and the anti-institutionalism of nonconformism, and instead seeks to develop a relationship with the world, not only as a distinct voice, but as a distinct partner. In this sense Christianity is not seen as another competing ideology in the contemporary world. Just as the church is enriched by the many groups in the world, these leaders present the faith as something that has a vital role in enriching the life of the world. Far from representing a loss of distinctiveness or integrity, this is an affirmation of the church and its faith in the public square, not only to proclaim what is believed, but also to share in wrestling with the many unresolved questions and concerns of the world.

The carefully defined courses of Rollins's nonconformism and Milbank's radical orthodoxy are, undoubtedly, deeply attractive in such a fast and furious world. I do believe, however, that there is integrity in the positions that the church leaders are maintaining. While it is not as obvious as radical orthodoxy or 'liquid church', there is a shared character trait that appears to run through what the different church leaders express.

This is no more specific than a commitment to remain both open to the world and faithful to the inherited faith and church. While one could easily say that such a general statement is true of any church or leader, I use the statement within the context of the church as I have explained it, existing between three sets of tensions. To be conservative evangelical, postmodernism must be wrong; to be radically orthodox, postmodernity must be wrong; to be nonconformist, institutionalism must be wrong. What the church leaders embody is not so much a confused middle ground but a way of being faithful, without closing oneself off from the possibility that something good might come from today's Nazareth,[57] that is, the postmodern condition.

The understanding of the faith and the church that I am observing is simply that they cannot grow if they are shut away from the world. Any attempt to keep the church separate from the world denies the reality of its own existence as being a part of the world. This is something that the theologian David Tracy calls 'critical correlation'. This approach suggests that the church has always existed in a critical dialogue with its wider setting, as a particular group among the many groups that make up 'the world'. This is further emphasized when one thinks of the people who make up the church: not only are they members of other groups, but they have always existed in a context where they belonged to more than one group. For as soon as a person is born, he or she is exposed not only to multiple points of view, but also to multiple ways of thinking about the world. Dialogue between these different ideas and ways of thinking is simply a part of the landscape in which all of humanity is raised and learns to navigate. It should not be a surprise, then, that all groups and institutions – including the church – are formed in dialogue with other groups, as well as in dialogue with their own histories. I will explain this further in my final chapters, as I seek to demonstrate that those living within the tensions of today's church and world are far from confused, faithless or apathetic; rather, they are attempting to inhabit space and time in a way that honours the faith and the church they have inherited, and that is redemptive for the postmodern condition.

5

The church: a very public inheritance

———•·•·•———

The church's relationships with the thinking, the cultures and the institutionalism of the postmodern condition are marked by a tendency for either conflict, populism or dialogue. Those thinkers and groups at the 'poles' of these relationships either refuse to engage at all, or allow the postmodern condition too much influence. The church leaders with whom I have met reject these two options, instead modelling forms of dialogue that attempt to engage critically with the faith and practices they have inherited, as well as with the contemporary world. It is my hope that using the labels of conflict, populism and dialogue will help the church to move away from the inappropriate definitions of 'inherited' or 'emerging' currently in use. In the previous chapter I outlined the theories behind the relationships that tend towards conflict, populism and dialogue. In this chapter, I will explain what these relationships look like and why I believe a tendency towards dialogue should always be the preferred option.

The church-in-conflict

The notion of the church-in-conflict emphasizes that the church is so different from a particular setting that it will lose its soul if it enters into dialogue: 'no negotiation with terrorists' is the style of response. This can be seen in radical orthodoxy's treatment of postmodernity, Rollins's view of the institutional church and Carson's condemnation of postmodernism. Such rejection naturally causes conflict, which is reflected in the language they use to speak of their vision. I have already given some brief examples of this in Chapter 2, such as Davison's and Milbank's patronizing treatment of the practices of Fresh Expressions, and Doug Gay's anti-institutionalism. It will be helpful to give a more detailed example of this kind of approach, by explaining and examining the conflict approaches of Stanley Hauerwas and N. T. Wright.

Stanley Hauerwas

Since around 1985, the concept of the church as a colony that exists in opposition to the nations has gained enormous support, almost solely through the work of American theologian Stanley Hauerwas. As he was beginning his writing, the dominant style of ethics and public theology in the USA was hugely influenced by H. Richard Niebuhr, who encouraged a dialogue between the state and the church. Hauerwas, who had been influenced by the idea that the Christian big story was far too distinctive to allow the church to enter into this kind of relationship with the state, claimed that Niebuhr was simply underwriting liberal democracy with a bit of theology.[1] The most positive result Hauerwas could think of from this project was that it simply made America a bit 'nicer';[2] clearly, this dialogue was a dead end for the church.

The big story that runs through all of Hauerwas's work has been inherited from the pacifist and Anabaptist writings of John Howard Yoder. For Hauerwas, the church began as a colony, distinct from the nations, during Jesus' Sermon on the Mount. This colony is said to have been formed by those who came out of the crowd in order to be disciples of Jesus.[3] People joined the colony by believing that Jesus, not Caesar,[4] was Lord, and by committing themselves to non-violence, because to be disciples of Jesus was to follow his path of non-violence, even unto death.[5] As the church developed, however, it entered into a settlement with the Emperor Constantine, in which the church lost its soul. Rather than remembering and enacting its tradition, which began at the Sermon on the Mount, the church reflected upon its position on the basis of 'how much Christian ethics Caesar [could] be induced to swallow without choking'.[6] The church, according to Hauerwas, has ever since found itself in a constant battle between faithfulness to the big story and accommodation to the nations. Hauerwas calls the church to separate itself from giving loyalty to the nations, and so remember again its role as a community that does not require war for its self-understanding and to make real its future desires.[7]

Hauerwas's writing is immensely convincing, and there is something terribly appealing about a church that lives so peaceably in the here and now. That, however, is only to accept one part of Hauerwas's big story, for while it defines the church in romantic technicolour, it defines 'the world' very differently. For Hauerwas, the world is comprised of nation states, each with their own Caesar on the throne. Whether they are dictatorships or democracies, all nation states reserve the right to militarize their citizens and subjects, in order to kill other human beings.[8] While Hauerwas is often accused of tribalism, he claims that it is in fact the nation states that tribalize humanity and claim an allegiance that is neither deserved nor earned.[9] For a Christian to fight on behalf of a nation is not only to be prepared to kill other humans, even Christians, but, at a deeper level, it is to forget that Christ, not Caesar, is Lord. Hauerwas simply cannot accept that any official engagement between the church and the state is anything other than the co-opting of the church by the state to further the purposes of

Caesar.[10] There can be no settlement or compromise as the big stories are too different. The nations are in conflict with the church, and this is the way it has always been.[11] There can only be one Lord – Caesar or Christ – and as with the first crowd hearing the Sermon on the Mount, a choice must be made.[12] Herein lies the formation of the colony, made up of those who see the truth of God in this story and so learn to live as 'resident aliens within a hostile environment'.[13]

Unlike many contemporary theologians, Hauerwas's enormous breadth of reading and interest is communicated with a dry, sometimes brash, always opinionated, wit that makes for an entertaining read. Often, even if one disagrees with him, the passion and enthusiasm with which he writes can raise the heartbeat. In this sense, Hauerwas is a deeply convincing writer, and as he tells 'the story' with such colour, one comes to realize that Hauerwas's work is rather like a very large novel. Indeed, reflecting upon the importance that novels have for him, Hauerwas comments that a good novel forces our eyes to move throughout the pages of the book, by which we become absorbed into a narrative world that 'gives us the skills to make something of our own lives'.[14]

Hauerwas's novel has two locations: the inhospitable and violent world, and the church, which is the oasis of salvation. This novel is utterly frightening and enchanting, and if Hauerwas's project is viewed in the same light as C. S. Lewis's Chronicles of Narnia or, perhaps more appropriately, Philip Pullman's His Dark Materials, then it becomes clear what Hauerwas is asking his readers to do. They are to learn his language, history and geography, and so learn how to be transformed from violence to peace. The problem here – and it is significant – is that this pacifist's novelizing of the world and the church employs rather violent means. Hauerwas's rhetoric collects the most difficult, degrading and delusory elements of liberal democratic life, and suggests that this is all the world has to offer. He ignores any sense of justice and development that has taken place within human society. Further, he appears to ignore the rather important question, raised by Nigel Biggar, as to what his idealistic, Christian politics would actually look like in reality, under the conditions of sin,[15] and indeed whether it would look any different from a liberal democracy. Put simply: is the world really that bad, and the church really *that* good?

N. T. Wright

While N. T. Wright also uses a big story approach, he is less damning of the world than Hauerwas, and believes the church should continue in its engagement with the state. This view, however, retains a sense of conflict as his understanding of the Christian big story is used to confront the many other stories that he sees making up the contemporary world, particularly the arrogance of political empire.

Wright believes that underlying the way any person looks at the world is a single, coherent big story that enables them to locate themselves in the world.[16] This belief leads Wright to understand Christianity as one, particular and discrete, worldview among many other big stories. This Christian big story is not Wright's invention, but the true story of the Bible itself, and the one to which Jesus constantly made reference.[17] Simply put, this big story is formed in five acts: Creation, Fall, Israel, Jesus and Judgement.[18] The driving force throughout this story is that God intends to renew creation and, to this end, Jesus Christ came as the fulfilment of Judaism and judgement of paganism. The announcement that emanates from the story is that the exile is over, and Yahweh, not Caesar, is on the throne.[19]

Along with Hauerwas, Wright believes that a Christian worldview is expressed through the choosing of one's Lord – Caesar or Jesus – and there appears to be no middle ground between the two. How the Christian person can exist within kingdom and empire, a hugely important question for the early Christian church, has all of its complexities reduced by Wright to being a matter of a very clear choice: either one is manifestly in the empire, or simply Christian in the kingdom.[20]

This understanding of being Christian is more fully worked out in *Virtue Reborn*,[21] in which Wright states that being Christian is about being 'formed by this capital-S Story'.[22] Virtue, which Wright understands as one's 'true' character,[23] is developed as one follows Jesus and thus learns to play one's part in the true 'Story'.[24] For Wright, faith and discipleship only make sense from within the big story; a person will never 'get it' until they come in and give it a try. Discipleship is understood as a process of crucifying those worldviews that are not Christian, and seeing them 'resurrected' within the framework of the big story.[25]

While his argument about a narrative basis to one's worldview is, in part, very helpful, Wright overstates the case by insisting that this is always a single, coherent story.[26] First, 'worldview' is surely more complicated and fluid than a single story; it is rather a baffling collection of many ways of looking at the world, which have been received throughout one's life. Sources of one's worldview can be seen in parents and family, school and neighbourhood, television, books and media, places of holiday and work, chance encounters . . . and this is only the beginning of the list. As well as the influence other people have upon a person, there are also interior sources, not least the chemical make-up of one's brain, and how that impacts the way a person understands the world. The development of human views and characters is far too complicated to be conveyed within a single story, no matter how big it is.

My second concern is that this big story is not as clearly demonstrated within the Bible itself as Wright insists. While the idea of 'Jesus versus Caesar and Satan' is certainly present within the New Testament texts, it is not all there is. As the New Testament scholar James Dunn has suggested, it seems that this big story dominates Wright's work in such a way that it is 'squeezing out' other important elements of discipleship within the New Testament. In particular, Wright ignores the relationship between righteousness and sinfulness, which occupied a great deal of St Paul's time.[27] Dunn points out that a good example of 'the kind of politics that Paul operated with is in the household instructions in Colossians',[28] where the apostle explains how slaves should be treated, without any sense that slavery itself could be wrong. Where Wright insists that the big story is the way humanity can join God in confronting the powers of the world, Dunn suggests that engagement between one's faith and one's culture has always been much more subtle than that.

What is unique to Wright, however, is his much more positive stance towards society, compared to that of Hauerwas. While his hope is that people will be rescued into God's kingdom, it is with the purpose that they will become agents in God's mission. Salvation is not simply a call to leave the world until Jesus returns, but to find one's place within the unfolding story as an agent of God's kingdom. A consequence of being nurtured in the story is that a person will become more involved in seeking to usher in the new Creation. For Wright, this necessarily involves work towards non-violent justice with individuals, governments and revolutionary groups, as this is all part of what it means to live under the lordship of the one who will return to 'put everything to rights'.[29] Wright sees no other way for the Christian person to live in the world except by involvement with the political authorities, and, unlike Stanley Hauerwas, he believes that there is a divine ordering to governments and authorities in order to uphold justice.[30] While one's affiliation is to Christ alone, this does not lead to any hint of moving to the edges of society, but rather to being involved in the central and institutional spheres.

Such engagement is certainly welcome, and may be one of the reasons why Wright's work is so popular among certain groups in the emerging church movement. The way Wright connects environmentalism with his big story, which moves towards inhabiting a New Creation, certainly chimes well with many within the emerging church movement. However, these churches should be aware that the underlying commitment to 'the big story' is far more conflictual and exclusive than they may realize. To agree with Wright's big story is also to agree with his assumptions, namely that other understandings of the Bible are less than adequate, there is a single big story running through the Bible, and salvation is only for those who have decided to enter into this big story.

There is no doubt that the church-in-conflict offers a very clear vision of the nature of the church: it knows its narrative, it knows what is right and what is wrong, who is in and who is out, how to get in, who should lead and who should not, and exactly what it needs to be doing. While it might take a little while to get to know some of the intricacies of the language and practices, the sense of clarity, purpose and belonging one gains from inhabiting such a community will be worth it. Such groups seem particularly inviting in times of great questioning and pursuit of change, such as the early twenty-first century, not because they make things 'simple' (radical orthodoxy and pyro-theology are far from 'simple') but because there is a sense of security and logic when living in their narratives. I believe that the price of such certainty, however, comes at the cost of reducing the complex nature of truth and one's perception of reality to a brand. Big stories are simply unable to sustain the kinds of claims they are used to make. As much as a person might yearn for clarity, is it worth the blinkers that one must wear in order for its claims to hold? Further, does the church really want to be *just another brand* in a world saturated with brands that rarely deliver their promises?

The church-in-dialogue

I believe there is a greater degree of openness within the theology and practices of the church leaders I have met than there is in Wright's big story, Hauerwas's anti-nations approach, radical orthodoxy's Christendom, or Rollins's pyro-theology. Dialogue, rather than conflict, appears to be a far more accurate way of describing the approach of many churches who are engaging in the postmodern condition. There is integrity in this dialogue: it is less about confusion or apathy, and more about resisting the kind of clarity embodied by the church-in-conflict. It is not that such clarity is necessarily bad, but that it may often come at the cost of the truth. Rather than 'standing firm' on one particular view of the church and the world, a form of dialogue is employed, the better to understand itself, the world and the relationships between the two.

There are many kinds of dialogue, and such a word can conjure up very different images, from the banal to the boisterous. The model that is most helpful here is David Tracy's 'critical correlation', albeit with a minor development. For Tracy, the theologian is the place in which critical correlation takes place, bringing the texts, people, practices and events of both the church and the wider world into a dialogue.[31] The foundation of this is not some desperate attempt for the church to remain relevant, but a theological conviction that because God is present throughout the world (i.e. the public), then talk about this God must also be in public; a dialogue with the whole world.[32] By bringing the church's faith and practices into dialogue with one's world, the theologian's hope is to speak more truthfully about both.

What is different here is that the location of this critical correlation is changed from the theologian to a particular church or group, so that their meetings and writings become manifestations of, and opportunities for, this dialogue. Critical correlation is apparent, for example, in Jonny Baker's (see p. 47) attitude towards postmodern society and culture. While he wishes to affirm that such a culture should be 'celebrated and affirmed' as God is as much present in that culture as in any other, he is not so accepting of postmodernity to ignore the idea that consumerism is 'one of the more depressing things around postmodern culture'. Here, then, one can see a refusal to reject postmodernity wholesale, as with radical orthodoxy, but without the naive acceptance that is part of Ward's liquid church.

One can also see this critical engagement in Winnie Varghese's (see p. 47) understanding of orthodoxy. She is comfortable with the idea that inherited orthodoxies and social patterns can be innovated, 'like a family might be queer', but she sees no reason why this means the church should be burned to the ground, as with Rollins's view that the church institution is an obstacle to true Christianity. Far from being a part of the problem, church structures and buildings are 'a sign of where our mission should be', and enable the church to have a voice that we can't have 'individually – we have it as an institution'.

Similarly, Roy Searle (see p. 48) is thankful for some of the insights of postmodern philosophy that have given him a framework in which to say, 'Actually, I'm not so sure.' This does not appear to have taken him into the kind of extreme relativism or cultural accommodationism of which Carson warns, but into living out a 'rule of life, [because] for us the gospel is quite a radical alternative life, and I think we engage with local culture by living quite alternatively and radically'. This is a nuanced position that seeks to form rules by which he may critically engage with the kinds of ideas and claims associated with modernism and postmodernism, as well as the faith and practices of the church.

Such dialogue in the church is not a recent invention but, Tracy argues, has been central to the developing church from its earliest origins to the present day. This is well illustrated in the work of James Dunn, particularly in his excellent book, *Jesus Remembered*.[33] As I have noted above, Dunn believes that applying the 'big story' approach to the Bible is inappropriate, as it forces out of the Bible certain elements that don't fit with the story. As an approach, it also wrongly assumes that there is some hidden pattern that simply needs constructing.[34] Rather, Dunn and Tracy perceive that the New Testament presents a range of interpretations of the person and event of Jesus Christ, and believe the texts have more to say with their differences intact than if they are forced into a false unity.[35] This is not diversity for diversity's sake; rather, it is recognition that what is recorded in the New Testament is not the actual event and person of Jesus Christ, but rather the writings of the shared memories of the various witnesses and first disciples.

One cannot read the New Testament, then, without entering into dialogue with the various memories of Christ that are told on those pages. In this sense, the church's proclamation of Christ is an invitation to join in a very long conversation that has found particular ways of speaking about the faith.[36] The first interpretations in the New Testament demonstrate the impact that Jesus had on the earliest individuals and groups. As such, they are also the classic memories about Christ and the earliest days of the church. They are normative in the sense that they furnish speaking about life through a particular person (Jesus Christ) and particular events (from his Incarnation to Ascension, and the resulting church). However, they are also limited, as they were written by people-in-context with only a partial view of the world. The New Testament cannot provide a specific answer to many contemporary issues simply because its authors could not have conceived of such questions. This view suggests, then, that the church should not be limited by the language and worldviews of the first writers, but only by the object of their fascination and transformation, which is Christ.

Just as the Bible did not drop out of heaven, but was written and edited by human communities, so the Bible is handed on through particular communities with specific traditions and contexts. Receiving the faith within a Plymouth Brethren meeting is very different from receiving the faith in a Roman Catholic church. Any dialogue that may, or may not, take place between the church and the wider world is governed by that particular church's understanding of authority, tradition and normativity. The way this often works is helpfully outlined by theologian David Brown in two of his works, *Tradition and Imagination* and *Discipleship and Imagination*.[37]

Brown understands the development of the church to have moved in positive and negative directions throughout its existence. As he follows through some of its developments, he concludes his two works by suggesting a set of criteria for judging the past and continued developments, which is not based upon how closely the developments remain to the supposed authorial intention of the texts.[38] Rather, he is quite comfortable with the notion that the church can, and indeed should, enter into dialogue with, and sometimes correct, the Bible, limited as it is to its own contexts.[39] There is then a requirement not simply to mimic and so repeat the mistakes of the past but to risk measuring the received tradition within one's own context. It is only through this dynamic, claims Brown, that any tradition can develop and continue to give life.[40]

The first set of criteria is an attempt to understand what the Bible appears to be saying, and how that 'sits' in one's own context. Historical, social-scientific and literary skills are all necessary if the Bible is to be read in a way that attempts to understand its editors, writers and protagonists. Brown then develops this point by suggesting that the concepts that are used within, and emerge from, the Bible should be judged by contemporary standards. Some may be uncomfortable with this, preferring to say that it is the Bible that judges one's own culture, not the other way around.[41] However, Brown is not saying that this should not be so; rather, he asserts that where social life has progressed from ancient times, outdated biblical concepts should be corrected. Christians do not need to dress like Jesus in order to follow him, nor do they need to add to their own prejudices by sharing the ancient cultural blinkers of St Paul. It is important to ask whether the ancient concepts in the Bible still make sense in the present context, and whether they are even morally acceptable.

Whereas the first set of criteria encourages an imaginative engagement with the Bible, the second set acts as a corrective, asking whether one's thinking remains on message with the Christian gospel. The first question Brown raises is whether these engagements are still focused on Jesus Christ as presented in the New Testament, as it is these proclamations that shape all future speaking about Christ.[42] The second question is how one's imaginative engagement with the Bible is understood by one's church. Brown notes that, by its nature, this creates conflict, as it always has done, but in doing so, this conflict is the engine by which the church may continue to develop in its pursuit of true belief.[43] The kind of conflict envisioned by Brown is less like the exclusive divisions of the church-in-conflict, and more like the natural result of working through disagreements in dialogue.

This conflict, however, is present within authoritative, sometimes authoritarian, structures, which at least function as conversation partners. In this context, holding lightly to one's interpretation is necessary as it is weighed by those in authority, whether that be a congregational understanding of the local body, or a more Catholic view involving bishops and synods.[44] If it is modified, or even rejected, the individuals involved can continue to remain faithful, either by submitting to the institutional view, or by continuing to attempt to reform the group to which they belong. This submission to the wider community is important in preventing the faith from becoming insular, and operative only on a personal or local level. This is often what is in danger of occurring when individuals move to gather together with like-minded people to form 'alternative' expressions of their church tradition. Such community-mindedness is also important if the institution is to develop. This most complex level of human interaction, carrying historical and pastoral burdens to sustain a broad community, is necessarily slow to be shaped. If it is to develop, as all institutions must, then it will only be through interaction with the individual and local embodiments of the tradition, reminding the bearers of authority that their office is not only to hold the tradition to its normative past, but also to seek its movement in the present and towards the future. While those in authority have a central role in embodying the tradition as it has been understood, they also bear office to make space for individuals to enter more deliberately into dialogue with the Christian tradition within a particular context.

The sources of the church-in-dialogue, then, are the same sources that make up the church-in-conflict. The reason for such a difference is that the latter uses the sources to form a coherent, particular story, the logic and practices of which are built up in conflict with other stories. Therefore, radical orthodoxy is divine, whereas postmodernity is godless; pyro-theology opens the way to the Christ event, whereas the institutional church obstructs the Christ event. The church-in-dialogue, however, engages the sources through a coherent, particular and open set of dialogues that informs the logic and practices of the church in such a way as to remain open to further development. It is not that the church-in-dialogue has no boundaries, as its dialogues function under the governance of a specific ethos and particular form of authority. This may be the authority of a bishop and a liberal Catholic ethos, as with Stephen Gerth (see p. 48), or the carefully chosen ethos of the Northumbria Community (see p. 48), who seek to discover 'how to sing the Lord's song in a foreign land' through availability and vulnerability.

The church-in-conflict despairingly offers the world and the church something it cannot deliver: a brand new alternative. The problem, though, is that there is no escaping the reality of the postmodern condition, and the best the church-in-conflict can do is act like a day spa, where people can be massaged with the right words and actions to help them make believe that they are not really a part of the big, bad world. This may be therapeutic for some, but it does a disservice to the God who became flesh and dwelt among us. The postmodern condition is partly a response to the mass disappointment with the Enlightenment: so many big projects, promises and plans came to a conclusion not in world peace, but in war. The church has at its disposal extraordinary gifts that have the potential to help people discover the deeper reality of the life they are barely living, and it is the church-in-dialogue that is able to share these gifts with its world.

6

Resisting the brand new church

———•◦•———

In this final chapter, I will outline ways in which the church-in-dialogue is transforming the world, not as an alternative to the world, but as a partner with a stake in the world's future. This discussion will be organized around five key issues that are prominent within the postmodern condition. 'Space' and 'time' in the postmodern condition have been compressed to maximize profit; 'stories' are mistrusted as never being able to live up to their own hype; 'popular media' exists to turn stories over in order to maximize viewer traffic and increase its market share; 'branding' presents an image that may or may not reflect the reality behind the glossy pictures and fluffy words. The church exists in this same world, and yet is able to lead people into a deeper understanding of the reality that these words both express and mask. This chapter will refer to explicit practices and ways of speaking that demonstrate the confidence and partiality, the knowledge and the hope, that are so constitutive of the Christian faith, which deepens through its engagement with others.

Space

The postmodern world is a crowded place. As populations continue to increase, so do their demands. This means more housing needs to be built, more cars will be driven around and more pressure will be placed on the various types of schooling and social care that states are trying to provide. Such demands will, in turn, increase pollution, making it even more difficult for already stretched healthcare systems to be effective. Alongside all of this, social and mobile media advances mean that we are never far from family, friends, colleagues and acquaintances, as we 'check in' and instantly upload thoughts and pictures from wherever we are in the world. While there are advantages to this, such technology causes us to live in a permanent crowd. The lack of space is both an external and internal problem, to which we need to adapt.

While I believe the theory of radical orthodoxy to be unnecessarily focused on conflict with the world, the kinds of practices suggested by Davison and Milbank are quite helpful. Their desire is to see a more confident and creative church, and I couldn't agree more with this. While some of their ideas sound rather twee, many of them are good ways for the church to inhabit the space in its locality. Outdoor services and processions, inviting community art groups to decorate one's hall, and intelligent use of churchyards are all good ways of demonstrating the sanctity of the world in which we all live. But the kind of crowding that is taking place – both externally and internally – demands much more than this, both in church buildings and services, and across the church's locality.

Worship: the offering of space

I have attended many seminars and lectures on 'worship in the contemporary world' and have been instructed on numerous occasions that the church must learn from the contemporary media in the way services of worship are conducted. While I believe there are lessons to be learned, I do wonder whether making the church look like the control centre of a television or radio station is really the best way of offering redemption in a crowded world. More than that, I see time and again that a good story, without pictures or props, told well, can hold a room together in a way that television rarely does. It is this, a story well told, that is at the centre of the church's worship.

It is interesting that the vast majority of participants with whom I met as part of this project shared in the Eucharist on a weekly basis. Many called it their 'main service', and that includes those from evangelical and 'free church' perspectives. While there are likely to be many reasons for this, I believe that part of it has to do with the way the Eucharist breaks people away from the crowdedness of the world and brings them into multiple locations.

The narrative itself takes the worshippers directly into the Upper Room, as Jesus confuses the disciples by offering himself to them in bread and wine; and so the congregation kneel or stand, not only looking on, but gathering with the first disciples, accepting this gift in faith without really understanding it. At the same time, this gathering around Christ in bread and wine fuses heaven and earth, so that the whole company of heaven, the living and the dead, are united in their common worship of Christ. Such connection through Christ also unites all of those on earth who are sharing in this 'one bread', even if they are physically separated. Finally, in receiving Christ in the bread and wine, communicants are taken into Godself, deeply into God's mysterious eternity, so that human time and space is lost as one becomes aware, however partially or fleetingly, of the richness and depth of the space that is to come.

Space is becoming an evermore luxurious commodity, yet the church has been given the gift of eternal space in the Eucharist. It is given, not only so that people might find their place in God, but that they might be enabled to allow God to make room in their own lives. It is impossible not to internalize the crowdedness of this world, and too easily people's lives are filled with non-stop action, so that living an examined life becomes less and less likely. At the Eucharist, as humanity enters into God, so God enters into each person to create room so that the gospel will take root, and those who receive Christ in Communion will share Christ in their lives. This is an extraordinary gift bestowed upon the church, and it offers not only good news to a crowded world, but also a challenge to reorder the way the postmodern world organizes life.

Community: the sharing of space

While they are neither new nor difficult, in terms of demonstrating what it means for all of God's people to live in the same space, focused community action projects can be very effective. Let me be clear: I am not suggesting that the church organize groups to go and paint fences and clean streets in order to look good in front of its neighbours. That approach to mission has far more to do with public relations than it does the gospel; I am not interested in convincing my neighbours that everyone in the church is a jolly, nice person, and that is where my neighbour, as a jolly, nice person, should also go. First, the church is not full of jolly, nice people; it is made up of human beings, each made in the image of God and each utterly flawed. Second, I don't think the church should be playing games to prove who has the best religion, as such an approach suggests that it is more interested in perception than it is in character.

The kind of community building I am talking about is where people of all faiths and none join together and do something. That's it. While the church might begin the process, it doesn't have to. This is simply about attempting to break down the barriers of the postmodern world and showing that people who happen to live in the same place, who walk past one another on a daily basis without saying a word, can actually be neighbours and companions. I don't think it requires a fanfare or branding, but simply organizing into a reality that slowly grows to be a regular part of community life. Often, it is churches that are well placed to begin the conversations that need to happen in order to make this a reality.

While litter tidying and graffiti washing are perfectly good examples of local action, they are not the only ways to engage in the postmodern space, which has been enormously affected by globalization. In one of my conversations with Jonny Baker, he shared a project that Grace has been involved in. West London sees a great deal of human trafficking for the purposes of the sex trade, and Grace partnered with other churches, charitable groups and state authorities to promote an educational campaign called 'The Truth Isn't Sexy'. Among other activities, specially designed beer mats were taken to pubs, with one side resembling a calling card, and the other telling the story of the person pictured. This is one way that a church was able to partner with other groups to deal with a global problem in their own locality.

What happens when non-sectarian community projects take place? Strangers become less common, and neighbourhoods are built, not because the streets are tidier, but because people have taken the opportunity to talk to one another. Through the church's involvement God ceases to be thought of as private, and the public reality of God becomes more visible. The church is no longer seen as a private-interest group, but as a genuine partner in the local community. The church also realizes that it is not as unpopular as it often thinks, finds a greater confidence to share what it has, and also learns from its neighbours.

Time

How can we live forever, when it is so patently obvious that we do not? This is, surely, one of the stickier questions for the church to get its head around. Yes, the church can talk about Christianity as a way to live a good life, a moral life, a religious life – but an eternal life? That's quite a claim, given the overwhelming evidence that all of life ends in the same way; we all live within time, and our experiencing of time ends with death. Actually, our attitude towards death, and what may be beyond, is linked to the way we think about time and our place within it.

This is less abstract than it may first seem. In one sense, time is simply a way of measuring one's steps through a finite life. For those who cannot conceive of anything beyond these finite bodies, time is all there is, and dying and death bring life to a close. Time therefore is short, and its fleeting nature causes human beings to try and make the most of what they have. Quality of life becomes focused on quantity of life; the more one can do, and the more days one has to do it in, the better one's life. This, of course, easily becomes intensely individualistic, so that what 'I' want becomes more important than the needs of others.

If time is fleeting and finite, what then of eternity? In speaking of eternity, the church needs to be careful not to suggest it is merely an escape from time, which is impossible; or a denial of time, which is futile; or that it is simply immortality, as if we will never die. Eternity is far more than these things.

The problem the church has in trying to speak of eternity is that it is as much 'within' time as anything or anyone else; we all see as 'through a glass, darkly' (1 Cor. 13.12 KJV). What enables the church to begin to speak of eternity is its belief in the resurrection. God's raising of Jesus Christ beyond life and death is an audacious shout that time is not the big story; there is yet more. This is to dare to say that time is not the ultimate reality, but belongs to an even wider reality, which is God's eternity. This wider reality is not completely out of our reach of knowing; it is a hope that is grounded in the sense of almost-knowing, which is that same drive that takes scientists to new discoveries and novelists to extraordinary creation.

Yet such is the audacity of this hope that it is almost unutterable: it seems almost cruel to share it in a world so marked by the disappointment of time cut short, as it so often is. Such hope of life beyond this life and death is, as T. S. Eliot said, the 'barely prayable prayer'.[1] And yet this is the faith and challenge that the church lays down to itself and the whole world: to live in the deeper reality of eternity, while being all too aware of the finite and frail reality of time. Life will end, and yet it will be transformed.

While I disagree with their view that the world experiences merely flux while the church experiences the 'fullness' of time, Davison and Milbank are quite right to show the importance that the church calendar has in rooting people in a deeper sense of reality. As Davison and Milbank state, the fasting of Advent and the Christmas light in the winter darkness, the springtime of Easter, the death of the year on All Saints and All Souls all help humanity understand its place within the natural rhythms of the world, as well as in the eternity that lies beyond this time.[2]

In addition to the calendar, Sue Wallace (see p. 47) also spoke about the importance that the communion of the saints holds for her two churches in their understanding of time. The communion of the saints reminds you that

> you're standing on the shoulders of giants. You're building on what has gone before, but you're also preparing for people who come after. In that sense your vocation isn't just your vocation; you're holding that baton and then you're going to pass it on. But also in the sense of wider community: it's people rooting for us with some who've been there before; you're part of the Christian community that actually stretches across time as well as across geography.

The church-in-dialogue does not attempt to avoid or escape time. It lives within time, and bears the pains as well as the joys of such life. But it resists being shaped by the lie that time is all there is. Instead, it seeks to be shaped by the God who is beyond time, who is bringing all of creation into an endless union. Simply believing in this as a concept will never remove all fear of dying and death. The rooting affect of the Christian calendar, and the celebration of God with his saints, gently moves the church from mere belief to trust, which is the beginning of living life according to the light of eternity, rather than the lengthening shadows of time.

Death is certainly the end of one's time, and it is a terrible separating from those with whom a person has shared life and love. Death leaves a gap that cannot be filled, and nothing can change that. Through the audacity of the church's faith, however, death is not the very end; it is the moment in darkness before the ecstatic encore begins, and the music you have longed for is finally played.

Stories

On Halloween, in 1938, Orson Welles's adaptation of *The War of the Worlds* was broadcast live on radio, largely as a series of 'news reports'. While it was only ever 'just a story', it is reported to have taken on a life of its own. For many reasons, some of the people listening are reported to have believed that they were witnessing an actual Martian invasion: some fled their homes; others are reported to have travelled to the site in New Jersey where it was supposedly taking place. Stories are rarely 'just stories'.

Given the power of stories, I am concerned by those who would want to turn 'stories', and more specifically their own stories, into 'the big story', which is a particularly popular trend in the church at this time. Talk of the Bible as having an overarching narrative has become so commonplace that any questioning of it sounds like heresy. Yet is it really possible to observe a story that runs, not only through the easy headlines of Creation and redemption, but through the God-authored bloodlust and ethnic cleansing of the Old Testament, and the continued subjugation of women in the New Testament? In this context, using a big story in order to make sense of everything seems not only foolish (because it omits all kinds of important events and themes), but also profoundly arrogant. Perhaps another story can help me make sense of this.

Of all of his wonderful, multilayered novels, Umberto Eco's *Foucault's Pendulum* is, for me, his most dangerous, challenging and absorbing. It follows a group of book editors who, for many different reasons, use various unconnected myths to create a big story that is intended to make sense of everything. The results are tragic for all involved as the story takes on a power beyond itself. The one consistent voice of wisdom throughout the book is Lia, the only main female character, who warns her partner against his project. She understands the dangers involved in the seemingly innocuous inventing of big stories: 'People are starved for plans. If you offer them one, they'll fall on it like a pack of wolves. You invent, and they'll believe.'[3]

While Eco's criticism of big stories in this novel actually turns into a big story itself,[4] his warning stands: big stories do not liberate you; they consume you. This is the concern I outlined earlier from the work of Jean-François Lyotard: far from denying the existence of big stories, Lyotard is exhausted by the failure of big stories to deliver their claims. The church-in-dialogue shares this exhaustion, and rather than seeking the one big story to bind all stories, it attempts to hold various voices together in an attempt to speak of 'all things'. Stories, even big stories, are still present; but they are held in plurality and dialogue, rather than as a closed system.

The critical difference is whether one understands a story as closed or open. A closed story is all that is needed: it tells you who you are, where you're from and going, and what you need to do. You don't bring a great deal (if anything), but rather learn what you're supposed to do. You diminish under the power of the story. Some might argue that this is liberation, but it looks more like consumption to me. An open story is broader than a closed story, and is able to be held together with many different (sometimes conflicting) smaller stories. An open story is as filled with claims for truth and hope as is a closed story, but it knows that its knowledge of such claims remains partial, and will grow only through further questioning, exploring and living. An open story develops as people bring it into dialogue with other stories.

Jonny Baker explained this well in one of my meetings with him:

> So, minimally, I need to have humility around my truth-claims, and I think that's been backed up by the feeling that, in terms of theology, people have made truth-claims that have come undone, I suppose. They've been too arrogant and dominant.

Equally, Callid Keefe-Perry (see p. 47) demonstrated the idea that these open stories are a complex of many stories and always have more than one narrator, making them far more diverse and multilayered than a closed big story:

> If theology is the human response to the reception of grace, and postmodernism is the movement towards accepting marginalized voices, then there can be such a thing as postmodern theology. A postmodern theology would be a theology that is a response to the new things God is giving to the children of God, and dialectically hearing the way people are responding to it: this is the traditional perspective. This is how my conversation with that tradition can be explained, and how, given that my view is

different, we can work out what to do with that difference. The function of the postmodern theologian is far more about hosting a conversation that is ongoing than it is about concluding a conversation.

This is the church-in-dialogue at its most honest about the human condition. It doesn't seek to tie up all the threads of history into one pithy explanation, system or story. Rather, it is concerned with how its inheritance can help all people lead better lives within this biologically evolved, politically factious, endlessly brilliant and equally failing world. The church is one of the hosts of this dialogue, as well as being a partner with others, a guest in others and an outside voice with others.

Some churches have embodied this approach rather literally in their services: sermons have now been replaced by focused conversations that look at a specific Bible text or issue; the monologue approach to 'outreach' where one person preaches to a room of interested people is beginning to be replaced by less structured, group-led dialogues. In churches with a liturgical tradition, such openness has not been seen as a reason to jettison the bits of the service that feel less open. Rather, as Gray-Reeves and Perham (see p. 34) found, liturgical action is becoming more complex to account for the different ways in which those in the gathered congregation understand what is going on. The goal of a uniform understanding of one big story has been brought into question by the blatant differences that are always – and have always been – present in the church. This is certainly not unique to the postmodern condition and, as James Dunn has made clear, has been the case from the very beginning of the church. A single story is far too blunt – and human – an instrument to unite the church. More than that, a single story will only ever serve to simplify the teachings of Christ, pacify the character of Christ, limit the events of Christ and misrepresent the editing of the Bible. While the approach of the church-in-dialogue, with an open attitude to the truth and stories, may well be caricatured as woolly, it is surely the church-in-conflict, with its many certainties and systems, that comes at the cost of the truth.

Media

On the evening of 3 November 1864, biologist and supporter of natural selection Thomas Huxley had dinner with seven colleagues in London. This was the first meeting of the X Club, a society founded for the furtherance of science free from theological dogmas. Huxley, who became known as 'Darwin's Bulldog', used a combination of networking and high-profile public debates with conservative establishment figures from the Church of England to demonstrate that there has always been a conflict between religion and science. The message that came across was a clear choice between rational scientific enquiry and social progression, or ancient myths and social conservatism. If astrophysicist and theologian David Wilkinson has read his history of science correctly, Huxley orchestrated this whole movement and, in so doing, actually created the conflict method as a way of publicly discussing science and religion.[5] This method, of course, is the one still favoured by the media today, and not only with regard to religion.

Putting two people who disagree with one another in the same room, and letting them fight it out on air is, to be frank, a rather shallow way of opening up any form of dialogue. It is thought to be good sport, however. Imagine the excitement, then, at the announcement in 2012 that Rowan Williams and Richard Dawkins were to have a public debate on 'The Nature of Human Beings and the Question of Their Ultimate Origin'. This was surely a dream come true for the media: archbishop versus militant secularist. For those hoping for a good fight and lots of punchy one-liners, disappointment loomed. Perhaps the BBC summed it up most accurately:

> It was a curious clash. After all the talk of militant secularism, this was more like a family fight between people who spoke a similar philosophical language . . . There were no real knockout punches delivered, with God and the atheists leaving with honours even and without tempers being frayed.[6]

When faced with the many complex political, economic and sociocultural issues of today's world, the populist media often decides that the hoi polloi need sound bites rather than nuance, and conflict rather than conversation. In the face of this decision, personality and public relations become more important factors in attracting support than evidence and arguments. While I think it is good for the church to be present within this kind of media, it needs to be very careful not to become just another part of the crowd, offering sound bites in an attempt to get noticed. A place in the media is important, but a place away from such a crowd is perhaps more so in terms of communicating the gospel.

The church that is comfortable with difference, dialogue and learning from others is a prime place and network in which to offer the opportunity to explore issues of contemporary life. Churches are often connected with all kinds of people and institutions, so that devising programmes on, for example, economics, politics or faith is a realistic option. In offering such opportunities to its local community, the local church needn't feel restricted to following the populist conflict model. Rather, the church can bring together like-minded (but not cloned) people who wish to seek a way forward on a particular issue. As well as holding lectures and seminars, it can also create opportunities to meet with local public servants, such as politicians and police officers, to discuss not only immediate needs, but also how such people can be better supported by the community in which they work.

Branding

Given that the brand is usually a person's first point of contact with a product or company, it is important that it tells that person everything he or she needs to know. When a product or company begins to wane in the popularity stakes, then the refreshing of its brand is taken very seriously as the way to enable the company to reach out to its target audience. Given that the church in the postmodern West is not growing, it is not difficult to understand why some believe that the church needs to refresh its brand.

For all of the claims for it as a new way of being the church, Fresh Expressions is basically a way of rebranding and reorganizing what the church has always done. Fresh Expressions is built upon the assumption that today's society has changed so dramatically that the church in its current form is no longer able to be present for the people it is called to serve. This, though, is a very big assumption built on very little evidence; it is fairly undeniable that the world has changed quite dramatically in the last century, but has it really left the church behind? That was certainly the view of secular theorists in the 1960s and 1970s, but the rise of religion in the world would suggest they were overstating their case. Rather than taking time to investigate this properly, the Methodist Church and Church of England have given in to a sense of panic, believing that a new way of organizing ministry (much of which already existed in some form or another) is the way forward.

Far from saving the church, this rebranding has placed new burdens upon the resources of people and finance, and is in danger of demotivating and alienating the clergy and ministers who are not a part of the Fresh Expressions networks. Suggesting that a person might be gifted to be a 'pioneer' rather than a 'traditional incumbent' is a terrible turn of phrase, as all of the church's ministers need to be pioneering. Parish priests and Methodist circuit ministers did not respond to God's calling simply to manage a church in its final years of decline. Yet that is often the understanding that emanates from Fresh Expressions writing (wittingly or not). Let me be clear: the kinds of ministry that take place under the banner of Fresh Expressions appear to be very good. It is the banner itself that is an unnecessary bureaucracy. The impact of the Church of England's *Mission-Shaped Church* report should not have been to create a new layer of bureaucracy, but to help all parish churches realize their missional calling, and to train incumbents and ministers to manage better and release lay people into local ministry. Such releasing would include allowing lay people to pioneer and lead groups that reach various networks of local people, while incumbents and ministers supervise and encourage those involved.

I do not accept that the answer to the woes of the church and the world lies in a new brand and an increase in bureaucracy. Nor do I believe, as Rollins does, that institutions and buildings block the way to the Christ event. Neither can I go along with Ward's suggestions that the church allow its geographical and parochial structures to be replaced by networks of like-minded people who gather around particular brands of church politics, each of which have their own charismatic leaders. While this may be how the church often functions, it should not be the church's vision to exist in such a consumerist manner. Finally, while I agree with Davison and Milbank that the church should have the confidence and poise to be able to serve the world according to its calling, this should not be done in such a way that denigrates the world and makes a fantasy of the church.

I believe Winnie Varghese put this very well during my meeting with her at St Mark's Church in central Manhattan:

> Buildings in the city are not a mistake: they are a sign of where our mission should be. We cannot abandon the city, because we have these buildings; they are a gift. The money is there, the people are there, the energy is there. The problem is: can we believe in ourselves enough to actually be the kind of community God calls us to be as church? It involves a level of discipline, and discernment and help that can be counter-intuitive when you're trying to live out the passion and drive that God gives you to be who you are: building up the least among us so that you can have space for people who don't have space, to be with the broken. This church does all of those things very well [with] the marginal of the marginal.

I entirely agree with Winnie, but would go even further: as well as being signs of 'where our mission should be', church buildings are a part of that mission. It is not simply what takes place within the buildings, but the architecture itself that moves people to discover their lives being lived in time and in eternity. Far from being a way of hiding from the reality of the faith and the world, as Rollins suggests, church architecture draws people into the glory of God and the responsibility of being human.

Allow me to explain, by imagining yourself entering into a church building. Feel the stone of the walls and wood of the pews; observe the beauty of the material, the way it has been carved by hand; but also notice how it is hard and uncompromising to touch. Now look up at the windows, made of a material of a completely different order from that of stone and wood. The translucent light doesn't draw us in simply to look at it, as with the wood and stone, but to look through it.

We can stand in its projection of colours and images on the floor, even in the air around us. Anyone who has been to the Sainte-Chapelle in Paris will know the experience of 'breathing' the coloured air.

If only life were more like the order of light and colour than that of wood and stone. Yet I know that the way I see, and the way those around me see, is rather heavy and opaque. I sometimes feel that St Paul was being generous when he wrote, 'we see through a glass, darkly' (1 Cor. 13.12 KJV). So often, seeing life as it is can feel like banging my head against the wall.

The glass, so often filled with images of the saints, speaks of that different order of light and beauty. It is no accident, then, that as one approaches a high altar at the east end of many churches, the stone, wood and glass also gather: these orders are very deliberately being brought together. It is here that Christ is not only proclaimed, but also made manifest. It is not only that he is brought into our presence, but that we, in our order of wood and stone, somehow undergo a shifting into his presence. It is as we focus upon his presence alone that the orders of this life and of glory are united in their worship of Christ. Every time we share in the Eucharist, we are given a glimpse of the unity that is promised in Christ; that one day, all things in heaven and earth will be brought together, and will find their peace in the God who creates and sustains all things.

This is the power of the church's architecture. While there is nothing wrong with informal meetings and discussion groups in pubs and cafés, they can never carry the sense of transcendence in the same way as worship in a deliberately designed church. The church does not need rebranding, but a renewed confidence in that which it has inherited, that the whole world might come 'to comprehend with all the saints what is the breadth and length and height and depth, and to know the love of Christ that surpasses knowledge, that you may be filled with all the fullness of God' (Eph. 3.18–19).

The church in the postmodern condition

Creating space, revealing eternity, exploring truth, challenging conflict and resisting branding are all part of the way in which the church is already sustaining and deepening the dialogues that need to take place if the world is to understand itself better. People are often too ready to sit back and bemoan the fact that postmodern society is somehow broken, but not so ready to do something about it. The church is called to use its rich inheritance so that the people of this world might step out of the crowds. In this place of dialogue, men and women are given the opportunities to discover the way their lives are being dominated by certain big stories, and so encounter ways of being human that, in the noise of the crowd, were unimaginable.

Far from being a call out of the world, as its proponents claim, the church-in-conflict relies far too heavily upon the same strategies as the more cynical aspects of the postmodern condition. Calling people to live within a big story that is intended to dominate every aspect of their thinking and moving in this world does not bring about salvation. Quite the opposite: it mimics the patterns of other institutions, corporations and the media in attempting to gain a person's soul. The church is not in the business of collecting souls, but rather has a vocation of nurturing them.

The church began with the shared memories of a group of people who were convinced that the events around Jesus Christ that they had witnessed were not simply a good secret for them, but also somehow good news for the world, even for the Gentiles. The members of the church-in-dialogue continue this mission, not building private societies that condemn the world to hell, but faithfully speaking and practising their flawed understanding of faith in public for the flourishing of all God's people. This is the church in the postmodern condition, and it is not brand new.

Notes

1 Why bother with the postmodern condition?

1 Cf. N. T. Wright, 'The Christian Challenge in the Postmodern World', *Response* 28:2 (2005) <www.spu.edu/depts/uc/response/summer2k5/features/postmodern.asp>, last accessed on 28 August 2012.

2 David Lyon, *Postmodernity: Concepts in Social Thought* (Buckingham: Open University Press, 1999), 60.

3 Jean Baudrillard, *Simulacra and Simulations*, trans. Sheila F. Glaser, The Body, in Theory: Histories of Cultural Materialism (University of Michigan: University of Michigan Press, 1981), 75–7.

4 David Harvey, 'Postmodern Morality Plays', *Antipode* 24:4 (1992), 300–26 (300).

5 David Harvey, *The Condition of Postmodernity: An Enquiry into the Origins of Cultural Change* (Oxford: Blackwell, 1990), 62.

6 David Lyon, *Jesus in Disneyland: Religion in Postmodern Times* (Oxford: Polity, 2000), 127.

7 Harvey, 'Morality Plays', 322.

8 Harvey, 'Morality Plays', 316.

9 Harvey, 'Morality Plays', 305.

10 Harvey, 'Morality Plays', 318.

11 Jean-François Lyotard, *The Postmodern Condition: A Report on Knowledge*, trans. Geoff Bennington and Brian Massumi (Manchester: Manchester University Press, 1984), xxiv.

12 Lyotard, *Postmodern Condition*, 82.

13 Lyotard, *Postmodern Condition*, 60–1, 66.

14 Lyotard, *Postmodern Condition*, 81.

15 Lyon, *Postmodernity*, 56.

16 Jean-François Lyotard, 'That Which Resists, After All', *Philosophy Today* 36:4 (1992), 402–17 (403).

17 Lyotard, *Postmodern Condition*, 81.

18 Lyon, *Postmodernity*, 43.

19 Lyon, *Postmodernity*, 41.

20 Lyotard, *Postmodern Condition*, 81.

21 Madeleine Bunting, 'Passion and Pessimism', *The Guardian*: Review section, Saturday 5 April 2003, 20.

22 Zygmunt Bauman, *Identity*, Themes for the 21st Century (Cambridge: Polity, 2004), 51.

23 Lyon, *Postmodernity*, 86.

24 Bauman, *The Art of Life* (Cambridge: Polity, 2008), 29–30.

25 Bauman, *Art of Life*, 23.

26 Bauman, *Art of Life*, 51–92.

27 Bauman, *Art of Life*, 109.

28 Bauman, *Art of Life*, 105, original italics.

29 Bauman, *Art of Life*, 106, original italics.

2 Marmite for the church: the loving and loathing of the emerging church

1 Eddie Gibbs and Ryan K. Bolger, *Emerging Churches: Creating Christian Communities in Postmodern Cultures* (London: SPCK, 2006), 235.

2 Gibbs and Bolger, *Emerging Churches*, 157, 218, 236.

3 Gibbs and Bolger, *Emerging Churches*, 235.

4 Gibbs and Bolger, *Emerging Churches*, 242–3.

5 Gibbs and Bolger, *Emerging Churches*, 28.

6 Gibbs and Bolger, *Emerging Churches*, 96.

7 D. A. Carson, *Becoming Conversant with the Emerging Church: Understanding a Movement and Its Implications* (Grand Rapids, MI: Zondervan, 2005), 76.

8 Carson, *Becoming Conversant*, 45.

9 Carson, *Becoming Conversant*, 15.

10 Carson, *Becoming Conversant*, 24.

11 Carson, *Becoming Conversant*, 27, 59

12 Carson, *Becoming Conversant*, 51.

13 Carson, *Becoming Conversant*, 68.

14 Carson, *Becoming Conversant*, 126–32.

15 Carson, *Becoming Conversant*, 139–41. This complaint is also made by Davison and Milbank, below.

16 Carson, *Becoming Conversant*, 141–5.

17 Carson, *Becoming Conversant*, 146.

18 Carson, *Becoming Conversant*, 155–6.

19 Carson, *Becoming Conversant*, 184.

20 Carson, *Becoming Conversant*, 186.

21 Carson, *Becoming Conversant*, 45.

22 Carson, *Becoming Conversant*, 165–6, 181, 200, 213–14.

23 Carson, *Becoming Conversant*, 185–6.

24 Carson, *Becoming Conversant*, 230–3.

25 Carson, *Becoming Conversant*, 175.

26 Tom Sine, *The New Conspirators: Creating the Future One Mustard Seed at a Time* (Downers Grove, IL: IVP, 2008), 20.

27 Sine, *Conspirators*, 39.

28 Sine, *Conspirators*, 235.

29 Sine, *Conspirators*, 233.

30 Sine, *Conspirators*, 40–4.

31 Sine, *Conspirators*, 46–9.

32 Sine, *Conspirators*, 49–55.

33 Sine, *Conspirators*, 59–70.

34 Sine, *Conspirators*, 125.

35 Sine, *Conspirators*, 76.

36 Sine, *Conspirators*, 205.

37 Sine, *Conspirators*, 208.

38 Sine, *Conspirators*, 257.

39 Sine, *Conspirators*, 256.

40 Sine, *Conspirators*, 260.

41 Sine, *Conspirators*, 260.

42 Sine, *Conspirators*, 279, 281.

43 Andrew Davison and Alison Milbank, *For the Parish: A Critique of Fresh Expressions* (London: SCM, 2010), x.

44 Davison and Milbank, *For the Parish*, 1, 9.

45 Davison and Milbank, *For the Parish*, 84–5.

46 Pete Ward, *Growing up Evangelical: Youthwork and the Making of a Subculture* (London: SPCK, 1996), 203; Pete Ward, *Participation and Mediation: A Practical Theology for the Liquid Church* (London: SCM, 2008), 150–1.

47 Pete Ward, *Liquid Church* (Carlisle: Paternoster, 2002), 59–60.

48 Ward, *Liquid Church*, 16, 26–9, 41.

49 Davison and Milbank, *For the Parish*, 86.

50 Martyn Percy, 'Old Tricks for New Dogs', in Louise Nelstrop and Martyn Percy (eds), *Evaluating Fresh Expressions: Explorations in Emerging Culture* (Norwich: Canterbury Press, 2008), 31.

51 Davison and Milbank, *For the Parish*, 172.

52 Davison and Milbank, *For the Parish*, 130–1.

53 For a more in-depth introduction, James K. A. Smith, *Introducing Radical Orthodoxy: Mapping a Post-Secular Theology* (Grand Rapids, MI: Baker Academic, 2004). For a full discussion, John Milbank, *Theology and Social Theory: Beyond Secular Reason* (Oxford: Blackwell, 1990, 1993).

54 Cf. Milbank, *Theology*, 6, 388, 432; John Milbank, *Being Reconciled: Ontology and Pardon*, Radical Orthodoxy Series (Abingdon and New York: Routledge, 2003), 128–9, 196.

55 Davison and Milbank, *For the Parish*, 124–6.

56 Davison and Milbank, *For the Parish*, 210.

57 Davison and Milbank, *For the Parish*, 102–5.

58 David Harvey, 'Postmodern Morality Plays', *Antipode* 24:4 (1992), 300–326 (300).

59 Kevin Corcoran (ed.), *Church in the Present Tense: A Candid Look at What's Emerging* (Grand Rapids, MI: Brazos Press, 2011), xi–xii.

60 Corcoran (ed.), *Present Tense*, xii–xiii.

61 Corcoran (ed.), *Present Tense*, xii–xiii.

62 Corcoran (ed.), *Present Tense*, xiii–xiv.

63 Corcoran (ed.), *Present Tense*, xiv.

64 Corcoran (ed.), *Present Tense*, xv.

65 Peter Rollins, 'The Worldly Theology of Emerging Christianity', in Corcoran (ed.), *Present Tense*, 25, 27; Jason Clark, 'Consumer Liturgies and Their Corrosive Effect on Christian Identity', in Corcoran (ed.), *Present Tense*, 41, 43, 52–3, 56.

66 Kevin Corcoran, 'Who's Afraid of Philosophical Realism? Taking Emerging Christianity to Task', in Corcoran (ed.), *Present Tense*, 3–4, 5–16, 19.

67 Peter Rollins, 'Transformance Art: Reconfiguring the Social Self', in Corcoran (ed.), *Present Tense*, 99.

68 Rollins, 'Transformance Art', 98–101.

69 Mary Gray-Reeves and Michael Perham, *The Hospitality of God: Emerging Worship for a Missional Church* (London: SPCK, 2011), 3.

70 Gray-Reeves and Perham, *Hospitality*, 4, 44, 79.

71 Gray-Reeves and Perham, *Hospitality*, 5.

72 Gray-Reeves and Perham, *Hospitality*, 17.

73 Gray-Reeves and Perham, *Hospitality*, 29–31.

74 Gray-Reeves and Perham, *Hospitality*, 32–3, 84.

75 Gray-Reeves and Perham, *Hospitality*, 62, 65.

76 Gray-Reeves and Perham, *Hospitality*, 18, 64, 141–2.

77 Gray-Reeves and Perham, *Hospitality*, 21.

78 Gray-Reeves and Perham, *Hospitality*, 18.

79 Gray-Reeves and Perham, *Hospitality*, 120.

80 Gray-Reeves and Perham, *Hospitality*, 119.

81 Gray-Reeves and Perham, *Hospitality*, 55.

82 Gray-Reeves and Perham, *Hospitality*, 107.

83 Gray-Reeves and Perham, *Hospitality*, 134–5, 138–41.

84 Gray-Reeves and Perham, *Hospitality*, 144–5.

85 Gray-Reeves and Perham, *Hospitality*, 69–70, 72, 72, 75, 78.

86 Gray-Reeves and Perham, *Hospitality*, 71.

87 Gray-Reeves and Perham, *Hospitality*, 136–7.

88 Gray-Reeves and Perham, *Hospitality*, 82–3, 87, 91, 121–2, 129, 132, 134, 146.

89 Gray-Reeves and Perham, *Hospitality*, 91.

90 Doug Gay, *Remixing the Church: Towards an Emerging Ecclesiology* (London: SCM, 2011), 3–5.

91 Gay, *Remixing*, 46–7.

92 Gay, *Remixing*, 48–9.

93 Gay, *Remixing*, 73.

94 Gay, *Remixing*, 93–4.

95 Gay, *Remixing*, 3 (n. 3).

96 Gay, *Remixing*, 74 (n. 1).

97 Gay, *Remixing*, 78. Gay often places emerging in opposition to what he calls 'institutional' churches; cf. Gay, *Remixing*, 17, 41.

98 Gay, *Remixing*, 93–4.

99 Gay, *Remixing*, 55 (n. 5). This comment is in response to the practice of priestly blessing.

100 Gay, *Remixing*, xii.

101 This is particularly telling in his treatment of John Milbank's work, describing it as a 'pompous . . . anglo-centric . . . unimpressive sneer at Emerging Church initiatives' and 'frankly snobbish'; Gay, *Remixing*, 29 (n. 21), 64 (n. 34).

4 Mapping the church in the postmodern condition

1 D. A. Carson, *Becoming Conversant with the Emerging Church: Understanding a Movement and Its Implications* (Grand Rapids, MI: Zondervan, 2005), 122–4.

2 Carson, *Becoming Conversant*, 88–92.

3 Carson, *Becoming Conversant*, 112, 114–15.

4 Carson, *Becoming Conversant*, 152; cf. 175.

5 Carson, *Becoming Conversant*, 165–6, 181, 200, 213–14.

6 Carson, *Becoming Conversant*, 230–3.

7 Carson, *Becoming Conversant*, 126–32; also, D. A. Carson, 'Maintaining Scientific and Christian Truths in a Postmodern World' <www.scienceandchristianbelief.org/articles/carson.pdf>, 18–20, last accessed on 20 March 2012.

8 Carson, *Becoming Conversant*, 97.

9 Carson, *Becoming Conversant*, 25.

10 Carson, *Becoming Conversant*, 92.

11 Carson, 'Maintaining Scientific and Christian Truths', 1, 15–17.

12 Peter Rollins, 'In Defense of Pirates (and Orthodox Heretics)' <http://peterrollins.net/?p=533>, last accessed on 20 March 2012.

13 Rob Bell, 'Rob Bell Interviews Pete Rollins' <www.oasisaudio.com/files/products/Insurrection_PDF.pdf>, last accessed on 21 March 2012.

14 Rollins, 'Defense of Pirates'.

15 Peter Rollins, 'On Why the Christian God Generates Particularly Good Atheists' <http://peterrollins.net/?p=82>, last accessed on 20 March 2012.

16 John Milbank, 'Knowledge: The Theological Critique of Philosophy in Hamann and Jacobi', in John Milbank, Catherine Pickstock and Graham Ward (eds), *Radical Orthodoxy* (London: Routledge, 1999), 23, 26.

17 Philosophy without theology 'will reach aporetic and nihilistic conclusions . . . philosophy left to itself, brings itself, as Heidegger saw, to its own end'; Milbank, 'Knowledge', 37 (n. 49).

18 Frederick Bauerschmidt, 'Aesthetics: The Theological Sublime', in Milbank, Pickstock and Ward (eds), *Radical Orthodoxy*, 209.

19 Bauerschmidt, 'Aesthetics', 214–16.

20 Milbank, Pickstock and Ward (eds), *Radical Orthodoxy*, 1.

21 Pete Ward, *Liquid Church* (Carlisle: Paternoster, 2002), 1.

22 Pete Ward, *Growing up Evangelical: Youthwork and the Making of a Subculture* (London: SPCK, 1996), 203.

23 Pete Ward, *Participation and Mediation: A Practical Theology for the Liquid Church* (London: SCM, 2008), 150–1.

24 Ward, *Liquid Church*, 59–60.

25 Ward, *Liquid Church*, 16, 26–9, 41.

26 Ward, *Liquid Church*, 90.

27 Ward, *Liquid Church*, 72.

28 Milbank, Pickstock and Ward (eds), *Radical Orthodoxy*, 2.

29 William T. Cavanaugh, 'The City: Beyond Secular Parodies', in Milbank, Pickstock and Ward (eds.), *Radical Orthodoxy*, 192–3.

30 Andrew Davison and Alison Milbank, *For the Parish: A Critique of Fresh Expressions* (London: SCM, 2010), 129–32, 172.

31 Davison and Milbank, *For the Parish*, 210.

32 Milbank, Pickstock and Ward (eds), *Radical Orthodoxy*, 4.

33 Cavanaugh, 'The City', 182.

34 Cavanaugh, 'The City', 194.

35 John Milbank, *Theology and Social Theory: Beyond Secular Reason* (Oxford: Blackwell, 1990, 1995), 5.

36 Milbank, *Theology*, 196.

37 Milbank, *Theology*, 387.

38 Milbank, *Theology*, 6.

39 Milbank, *Theology*, 388, 432.

40 Milbank, *Theology*, 381.

41 Stuart Murray is also an important voice in attempting to re-establish non-conformity in relation to institutionalism; cf. Stuart Murray, *Post-Christendom: Church and Mission in a Strange New World* (Carlisle: Paternoster), 2004.

42 Peter Rollins, 'The Revolutionary Potential of the Actually Existing Church' <http://peterrollins.net/?p=3426>, last accessed on 20 March 2012.

43 Peter Rollins in Kevin Corcoran (ed.), *Church in the Present Tense: A Candid Look at What's Emerging* (Grand Rapids, MI: Brazos Press, 2011), 97, 101.

44 Rollins, 'Revolutionary Potential'.

45 Peter Rollins, 'The Leader Who Doesn't Lead' <https://vimeo.com/18881568>, last accessed on 20 March 2012.

46 Katharine Moody, 'The Poet and the Critic: Transformation and Information' <www.katharinesarahmoody.tumblr.com/post/12068860482>, last accessed on 20 March 2012.

47 John Milbank, 'Stale Expressions', *Studies in Christian Ethics* 21:1 (2008), 117–128, 125.

48 Milbank, 'Stale Expressions', 126.

49 Milbank, 'Stale Expressions', 126.

50 Milbank, 'Stale Expressions', 126–7.

51 Davison and Milbank, *For the Parish*, 156.

52 John Milbank, 'Being Reconciled: Ontology and Pardon', in Milbank, Pinstock and Ward (eds), *Radical Orthodoxy*, 210–11; Milbank, *Theology*, 6, 380–1, 433; Milbank, 'Stale Expressions', 127.

53 Milbank, 'Being Reconciled', 128–9, 196; Milbank, *Theology*, 6, 388, 432.

54 Cavanaugh, 'The City', 195–7.

55 Zygmunt Bauman, *The Art of Life* (Cambridge: Polity, 2008).

56 Bauman, *Art of Life*, 66–91.

57 To refer to Nathanael's response when first hearing of a carpenter from Nazareth (John 1.46).

5 The church: a very public inheritance

1 Stanley Hauerwas and William H. Willimon, *Resident Aliens: A Provocative Christian Assessment of Culture and Ministry for People Who Know Something Is Wrong* (Nashville: Abingdon Press, 1989), 41.

2 Hauerwas and Willimon, *Aliens*, 40; Stanley Hauerwas, *Against the Nations: War and Survival in a Liberal Society* (Minneapolis: Winston Press, 1985), 122–3.

3 Hauerwas and Willimon, *Aliens*, 74–7.

4 Hauerwas, *Nations*, 128.

5 Hauerwas, *Nations*, 117, 129–30.

6 Hauerwas and Willimon, *Aliens*, 72.

7 Hauerwas and Willimon, *Aliens*, 62; Hauerwas, *Nations*, 1.

8 Hauerwas, *Nations*, 127.

9 Hauerwas and Willimon, *Aliens*, 156.

10 Hauerwas, *Nations*, 128–9.

11 Hauerwas and Willimon, *Aliens*, 155.

12 Hauerwas, *Nations*, 129. '[T]he overriding conflict of our time . . . is the conflict between those that would remain loyal to God's kingdom and those that would side with the world.'

13 Hauerwas and Willimon, *Aliens*, 97, 140.

14 Stanley Hauerwas, *Dispatches from the Front: Theological Engagements with the Secular* (Durham, NC and London: Duke University Press, 1994), 55–6; cf. Hauerwas, *A Community of Character:*

Toward a Constructive Christian Social Ethic (Notre Dame, IN: University of Notre Dame Press, 1981), 12–35.

15 Nigel Biggar, 'Is Stanley Hauerwas Sectarian?', in Mark Thiessen Nation and Samuel Wells (eds), *Faithfulness and Fortitude: In Conversation with the Theological Ethics of Stanley Hauerwas* (Edinburgh: T. & T. Clark, 2000), 159.

16 N. T. Wright, *The New Testament and the People of God*, Christian Origins and the Question of God, vol. 1 (London: SPCK, 1992, 2nd edn, 1993), 69–77, 122–6.

17 N. T. Wright, *Jesus and the Victory of God*, Christian Origins and the Question of God, vol. 2 (London: SPCK, 1996), 199–200.

18 Wright, *People of God*, 141–3.

19 Wright, *People of God*, 413, 405–6, 453; *Victory of God*, 648–51.

20 N. T. Wright and Marcus Borg, *The Meaning of Jesus* (London: SPCK, 1999), 218–22; N. T. Wright, *Following Jesus: Biblical Reflections on Discipleship* (London: SPCK, 1994), 67–70.

21 N. T. Wright, *Virtue Reborn* (London: SPCK, 2010).

22 Wright, *Virtue*, 6, 20, 25, 225.

23 Wright, *Virtue*, 24–5.

24 Wright, *Virtue*, 225.

25 Wright, *Virtue*, 233–4, 240.

26 Wright, *People of God*, 44–6, 76–7, 78–9, 132, 135.

27 M. M. Mathison (ed.), 'An Evening Conversation on Jesus and Paul with James D. G. Dunn and N. T. Wright', 25 October 2004 <www.ntwrightpage.com/Dunn_Wright_Conversation.pdf>, 15, last accessed on 28 August 2007.

28 Mathison (ed.), 'Evening Conversation', 24.

29 N. T. Wright, *Simply Christian* (London: SPCK, 2006), 193–4.

30 Wright, *Simply Christian*, 193–4.

31 David Tracy, *The Analogical Imagination: Christian Theology and the Culture of Pluralism* (New York: Crossroads, 1981), 24–7, 81, 340, 375, 446–55.

32 Tracy, *Imagination*, 51.

33 James D. G. Dunn, *Jesus Remembered*, Christianity in the Making, vol. 1 (Grand Rapids, MI: Eerdmans, 2003).

34 Tracy, *Imagination*, 396, 879. This is the way Tracy appears to understand his position on narrative, as is well demonstrated in Gary L. Comstock, 'Two Types of Narrative Theology', *Journal of the Academy of Religion* 25:4 (1987), 687–717 (688).

35 Tracy, *Imagination*, 113; Dunn, *Jesus Remembered*, 396, 893.

36 Tracy, *Imagination*, 236–7.

37 David Brown, *Tradition and Imagination: Revelation and Change* (Oxford: OUP, 1999); *Discipleship and Imagination: Christian Tradition and Truth* (Oxford: OUP, 2000).

38 Brown, *Tradition*, 226.

39 Brown, *Tradition*, 111.

40 Brown, *Tradition*, 106–10; *Discipleship*, 389.

41 Brown, *Discipleship*, 396–8.

42 Brown, *Discipleship*, 398–402.

43 Brown, *Discipleship*, 317, 404–5.

44 Brown, *Discipleship*, 334.

6 Resisting the brand new church

1 T. S. Eliot, 'The Dry Salvages', Four Quartets, *The Complete Poems and Plays* (London: Faber & Faber, 1969), 186.

2 Andrew Davison and Alison Milbank, *For the Parish: A Critique of Fresh Expressions* (London: SCM Press, 2010), 174–89.

3 Umberto Eco, *Foucault's Pendulum* (Vintage: London, 2001), 618.

4 Most notably: the world is 'a harmless enigma that is made terrible by our own mad attempt to interpret it as though it had an underlying truth'; Eco, *Foucault's Pendulum*, 95.

5 Cf. David Wilkinson, 'Hawking, Dawkins and the Matrix' <www.st-edmunds.cam.ac.uk/CIS/wilkinson>, last accessed on 28 August 2012.

6 Sean Coughlan, 'Rowan Williams and Richard Dawkins in Oxford Argument' <www.bbc.co.uk/news/education-17140107>, last accessed on 28 August 2012.

Bibliography

Astley, Jeff. *Ordinary Theology: Looking, Listening and Learning in Theology* (Aldershot: Ashgate, 2002).

Bader-Saye, Scott. 'Improvising Church: An Introduction to the Emerging Church Conversation', *International Journal for the Study of the Christian Church* 6:1 (2006), 12–23.

Baudrillard, Jean. *Simulacra and Simulations*, trans. Sheila F. Glaser, The Body, in Theory: Histories of Cultural Materialism (University of Michigan: University of Michigan Press, 1981).

Bauman, Zygmunt. *Community: Seeking Safety in an Insecure World*, Themes for the 21st Century (Cambridge: Polity, 2001).

Bauman, Zygmunt. *Identity*, Themes for the 21st Century (Cambridge: Polity, 2004).

Bauman, Zygmunt. *The Art of Life* (Cambridge: Polity, 2008).

Beaudoin, Tom. *Virtual Faith: The Irreverent Spiritual Quest of Generation X* (New York: Jossey-Bass, 1998).

Beaudoin, Tom. *Witness to Dispossession: The Vocation of a Postmodern Theologian* (Maryknoll: Orbis, 2008).

Bell, Rob. 'Rob Bell Interviews Peter Rollins' <www.oasisaudio.com/files/products/Insurrection_PDF.pdf>, last accessed on 21 March 2012.

Biggar, Nigel. *Good Life: Reflections on What We Value Today* (London: SPCK, 1997).

Biggar, Nigel. 'Saving the Secular', *Journal of Religious Ethics* 37:1 (2009), 159–78.

Bosch, David J. *Transforming Mission: Paradigm Shifts in Theology of Mission*, American Society of Missiology Series 16 (Maryknoll, NY: Orbis, 1992).

Braaten, Carl E. and Robert W. Jenson. *The Strange New World of the Gospel: Re-Evangelizing in the Postmodern World* (Grand Rapids, MI: Eerdmans, 2002).

Brown, David. *Tradition and Imagination: Revelation and Change* (Oxford: Oxford University Press, 1999).

Brown, David. *Discipleship and Imagination: Christian Tradition and Truth* (Oxford: Oxford University Press, 2000).

Brown, David. *Through the Eyes of the Saints: A Pilgrimage through History* (London: Continuum, 2005).

Bunting, Madeleine. 'Passion and Pessimism', *The Guardian*: Review section, Saturday 5 April 2003, 20.

Caputo, John D. and Mark Yount. *Foucault and the Critique of Institutions* (Pennsylvania: Pennsylvania State University, 1993).

Caputo, John D. *The Prayers and Tears of Jacques Derrida: Religion without Religion* (Bloomington, IN: Indiana University Press, 1997).

Caputo, John D. and Michael J. Scanlon. *God, the Gift, and Postmodernism* (Bloomington, IN: Indiana University Press, 1999).

Carson, D. A. *The Gagging of God: Christianity Confronts Pluralism* (Leicester: Apollos, 1996).

Carson, D. A. *Becoming Conversant with the Emerging Church: Understanding a Movement and Its Implications* (Grand Rapids, MI: Zondervan, 2005).

Carson, D. A. 'Maintaining Scientific and Christian Truths in a Postmodern World' <www.scienceandchristianbelief.org/articles/carson.pdf>, 18–20, last accessed on 20 March 2012.

Charmaz, Kathy. *Constructing Grounded Theory: A Practical Guide through Qualitative Analysis* (London: Sage, 2006).

The Church of England, The Archbishop's Council 2004, *Mission-Shaped Church: Church Planting and Fresh Expressions of Church in a Changing Context* (London: Church House, 2004).

The Church of England, Ministry Division, Mission and Public Affairs Division, Fresh Expressions, *Encouraging Ordained Pioneer Ministry* <www.freshexpressions.org.uk/sites/default/files/Encouraging%20 ordained%20pioneer%20ministry.pdf>, last accessed on 28 August 2012.

Coffey, Amanda. 'Review of *The Self We Live By: Narrative Identity in a Postmodern World* (Oxford, New York: Oxford University Press, 2000) by James A. Holstein and Jaber F. Gubrium', *Contemporary Sociology* 31:3 (2002), 294–5.

Comstock, Gary L. 'Two Types of Narrative Theology', *Journal of the Academy of Religion* 25:4 (1987), 687–717.

Corcoran, Kevin (ed.). *Church in the Present Tense: A Candid Look at What's Emerging* (Grand Rapids, MI: Brazos Press, 2011).

Cote, Richard G. *Re-Visioning Mission: The Catholic Church and Culture in Postmodern America* (New York: Paulist Press, 1996).

Croft, Steven (ed.). *The Future of the Parish System: Shaping the Church of England for the 21st Century* (London: Church House, 2006).

Croft, Steven and Ian Mobsby (eds). *Ancient Faith, Future Mission: Fresh Expressions in the Sacramental Tradition* (Norwich: Canterbury Press, 2009).

Davison, Andrew and Alison Milbank. *For the Parish: A Critique of Fresh Expressions* (London: SCM Press, 2010).

De Groot, Kees. 'The Church in Liquid Modernity: A Sociological and Theological Exploration of a Liquid Church', *International Journal for the Study of the Christian Church* 6:1 (2006), 91–103.

Dunn, James D. G. *Jesus Remembered*, Christianity in the Making, vol. 1 (Grand Rapids, MI: Eerdmans, 2003).

Eco, Umberto. *Foucault's Pendulum* (Vintage: London, 2001).

Eliot, T. S. 'The Dry Salvages', Four Quartets, *The Complete Poems and Plays* (London: Faber & Faber, 1969).

Featherstone, Mike. *Undoing Culture: Globalization, Postmodernism, and Identity*, Theory, Culture and Society (London: Sage, 1995).

Fiske, John. *Understanding Popular Culture* (New York: Routledge, 1989).

Flanagan, Kieran. 'Review of *Theology and Social Theory: Beyond Social Reason* (Oxford: Blackwell, 1990) by John Milbank', *British Journal of Sociology* 44:2 (1993), 360–1.

Gay, Doug. *Remixing the Church: Towards an Emerging Ecclesiology* (London: SCM Press, 2011).

Gibbs, Eddie and Ryan K. Bolger. *Emerging Churches: Creating Christian Communities in Postmodern Cultures* (London: SPCK, 2006).

Gordon, Avery F. 'Review of *Postmodernity: Concepts in Social Thought* (Buckingham: Open University Press, 1999) by David Lyon', *Contemporary Sociology* 25:1 (1996), 18–19.

Gower Street. 'An Interview with N. T. Wright', composed on 22 December 2004 <http://gowerstreet.blogspot.com/2004/12/interview-with-nt-wright-part-5-of-6.html>, last accessed on 16 March 2010.

Graham, Elaine and Stephen Lowe. *What Makes a Good City: Public Theology and the Urban Church* (London: Darton, Longman & Todd, 2009).

Graham, Elaine, Heather Walton and Francis Ward. *Theological Reflection: Methods* (London: SCM Press, 2005).

Gray-Reeves, Mary and Michael Perham. *The Hospitality of God: Emerging Worship for a Missional Church* (London: SPCK, 2011).

Harvey, David. *The Condition of Postmodernity: An Enquiry into the Origins of Cultural Change* (Oxford: Blackwell, 1990).

Harvey, David. 'Postmodern Morality Plays', *Antipode* 24:4 (1992), 300–26.

Hauerwas, Stanley. *A Community of Character: Toward a Constructive Christian Social Ethic* (Notre Dame: Notre Dame Press, 1981).

Hauerwas, Stanley. *Against the Nations: War and Survival in a Liberal Society* (Minneapolis: Winston Press, 1985).

Hauerwas, Stanley. *Dispatches from the Front: Theological Engagements with the Secular* (Durham, NC and London: Duke University Press, 1994).

Hauerwas, Stanley. *Wilderness Wanderings: Probing Twentieth Century Philosophy and Theology*, Radical Traditions Series (Boulder, CO: Westview Press, 1997).

Hauerwas, Stanley and William H. Willimon. *Resident Aliens: A Provocative Christian Assessment of Culture and Ministry for People Who Know Something Is Wrong* (Nashville: Abingdon Press, 1989).

Heelas, Paul, Scott Lash and Paul Morris (eds). *Detraditionalization: Critical Reflections on Authority and Identity* (Oxford and Cambridge, MA: Blackwell, 1996).

Holstein, James A. and Jaber F. Gubrium. *The Active Interview*, Qualitative Research Methods Series 37 (London: Sage, 1995).

Holstein, James A. and Jaber F. Gubrium. *The Self We Live By: Narrative Identity in a Postmodern World* (Oxford and New York: Oxford University Press, 2000).

Huyssteen, J. Wentzel van. *Essays in Postfoundationalist Theology* (Grand Rapids, MI: Eerdmans, 1997).

Kaufman, Gordon D. 'Conceptualising Diverse Theology', *Journal of Religion* 62:4 (1982), 392–401.

Levinas, Emmanuel. *Otherwise Than Being or Beyond Essence*, trans. Alphonso Lingis (Boston, MA: Kluwer Academic Publishers, 1978).

Lynch, Gordon. *Understanding Theology and Popular Culture* (Oxford: Blackwell, 2005).

Lyon, David. *Postmodernity: Concepts in Social Thought* (Buckingham: Open University Press, 1999).

Lyon, David. *Jesus in Disneyland: Religion in Postmodern Times* (Oxford: Polity, 2000).

Lyotard, Jean-François. *The Postmodern Condition: A Report on Knowledge*, trans. Geoff Bennington and Brian Massumi (Manchester: Manchester University Press, 1984).

Lyotard, Jean-François. 'That Which Resists, After All', *Philosophy Today* 36:4 (1992), 402–17.

Lyotard, Jean-François. *Postmodern Fables*, trans. Georges Van den Abbeele (Minneapolis and London: University of Minnesota Press, 1997).

McLaren, Brian D. and Tony Campolo. *Adventures in Missing the Point: How the Culture-Controlled Church Neutered the Gospel* (Grand Rapids, MI: Emergent YS/Zondervan, 2003).

Mathison, M. M. (ed.). 'An Evening Conversation on Jesus and Paul with James D. G. Dunn and N. T. Wright', recorded on 25 October 2004 <http://www.ntwrightpage.com/Dunn_Wright_Conversation.pdf>, last accessed on 28 August 2007.

Milbank, John. *Theology and Social Theory: Beyond Secular Reason* (Oxford: Blackwell, 1990, 1993).

Milbank, John. *Being Reconciled: Ontology and Pardon*, Radical Orthodoxy Series (Abingdon and New York: Routledge, 2003).

Milbank, John. 'Stale Expressions', *Studies in Christian Ethics* 21:1 (2008), 117–28.

Milbank, John, Catherine Pickstock and Graham Ward (eds). *Radical Orthodoxy* (London: Routledge, 1999).

Mobsby, Ian J. *Emerging and Fresh Expressions of Church: How Are They Authentically Church and Anglican?* (London: Moot Community, 2007).

Moody, Katharine. 'The Poet and The Critic: Transformation and Information' <www.katharinesarahmoody.tumblr.com/post/12068860482>, last accessed on 20 March 2012.

Murray, Stuart. *Post-Christendom: Church and Mission in a Strange New World*, After Christendom (Carlisle: Paternoster, 2004).

Nation, Mark Thiessen and Samuel Wells (eds). *Faithfulness and Fortitude: In Conversation with the Theological Ethics of Stanley Hauerwas* (Edinburgh: T. & T. Clark, 2000).

Nelstrop, Louise and Martyn Percy (eds). *Evaluating Fresh Expressions: Explorations in Emerging Church* (Norwich: Canterbury Press, 2008).

Newbigin, Lesslie. *The Gospel in a Pluralist Society* (London: SPCK, 1989).

Roberts, Richard H. 'Transcendental Sociology? A Critique of John Milbank's *Theology and Social Theory: Beyond Secular Reason*', *Scottish Journal of Theology* 46:4 (1993), 527–36.

Rollins, Peter. 'In Defense of Pirates (and Orthodox Heretics)' <http://peterrollins.net/?p=533>, last accessed on 20 March 2012.

Rollins, Peter. 'The Leader Who Doesn't Lead' <https://vimeo.com/18881568>, last accessed on 20 March 2012.

Rollins, Peter. 'On Why the Christian God Generates Particularly Good Atheists' <http://peterrollins.net/?p=82>, last accessed on 20 March 2012.

Rollins, Peter. 'The Revolutionary Potential of the Actually Existing Church' <http://peterrollins.net/?p=3426>, last accessed on 20 March 2012.

Silverman, David. *Interpreting Qualitative Data* (London: Sage, 3rd edn, 1993, 2006).

Sine, Tom. *The New Conspirators: Creating the Future One Mustard Seed at a Time* (Downers Grove, IL: IVP, 2008).

Smith, James K. A. *Introducing Radical Orthodoxy: Mapping a Post-Secular Theology* (Grand Rapids, MI: Baker Academic, 2004).

Smith, James K. A. *Who's Afraid of Postmodernism? Taking Derrida, Lyotard and Foucault to Church* (Grand Rapids, MI: Baker Academic, 2006).

Stackhouse, Max. 'Review of *Dispatches from the Front: Theological Engagements with the Secular* (Durham, NC and London: Duke University Press, 1994) by Stanley Hauerwas', *Christian Century* (18 October 1995), 962–7.

Stackhouse Jr, John G. *Humble Apologetics: Defending Faith Today* (Oxford: Oxford University Press, 2002).

Surin, Kenneth. 'Review of *Theology and Social Theory: Beyond Social Reason* (Oxford: Blackwell, 1990) by John Milbank', *Journal of Theological Studies* 44:1 (1993), 474–5.

Thiselton, Anthony C. *Interpreting God and the Postmodern Self: On Meaning, Manipulation and Promise* (Edinburgh: T. & T. Clark, 1995).

Tracy, David. *Blessed Rage for Order: The New Pluralism in Theology* (New York: Seabury Press, 1975).

Tracy, David. *The Analogical Imagination: Christian Theology and the Culture of Pluralism* (New York: Crossroads, 1981).

Turner, C. 'Zygmunt Bauman: Prophet of Postmodernity', *British Journal of Sociology* 51:4 (2000), 762–3.

Vanhoozer, Kevin J. *The Cambridge Companion to Postmodern Theology* (Cambridge: Cambridge University Press, 2003).

Volf, Miroslav. *Exclusion and Embrace: A Theological Exploration of Identity, Otherness and Reconciliation* (Nashville: Abingdon Press, 1996).

Walker, Andrew. *Telling the Story: Gospel, Mission and Culture* (London: SPCK, 1996).

Ward, Pete. *Growing up Evangelical: Youthwork and the Making of a Subculture* (London: SPCK, 1996).

Ward, Pete. *Liquid Church* (Carlisle: Paternoster, 2002).

Ward, Pete. *Participation and Mediation: A Practical Theology for the Liquid Church* (London: SCM Press, 2008).

Wilkinson, David. 'Hawking, Dawkins and the Matrix' <www.st-edmunds. cam.ac.uk/CIS/wilkinson/>, last accessed on 28 August 2012.

Wright, N. T. *The New Testament and the People of God*, Christian Origins and the Question of God, vol. 1 (London: SPCK, 1992; 2nd edn, 1993).

Wright, N. T. *Following Jesus: Biblical Reflections on Discipleship* (London: SPCK, 1994).

Wright, N. T. *Jesus and the Victory of God*, Christian Origins and the Question of God, vol. 2 (London: SPCK, 1996).

Wright, N. T. 'The Christian Challenge in the Postmodern World', *Response* 28:2 (2005) <www.spu.edu/depts/uc/response/summer2k5/ features/postmodern.asp>, last accessed on 23 March 2010.

Wright, N. T. *Simply Christian* (London: SPCK, 2006).

Wright, N. T. *Virtue Reborn* (London: SPCK, 2010).

Wright, N. T. and Marcus Borg. *The Meaning of Jesus* (London: SPCK, 1999).